Creating Space

How to design your calm, sane
and *outrageously gorgeous* home and
family-life

Niki Schäfer

New Age Publishers UK

Creating Space

To Richard, Genna, Finn and Zoë Grace and the calm, sane(ish), outrageously happy and gorgeous space we have created for our home and family.

For Jill Cartwright
L.Y.E.D.
x

MISSION STATEMENT

Niki Schäfer has written *Creating Space* to help women who are a little frustrated (or pulling their hair out) with their homes, to understand the surprising and positive impact their environment can have on their relationships, their esteem and the wellbeing of their family, so that they can create a home that truly reflects their personality and genuinely supports their wonderful, but let's face it, ridiculously busy lifestyle.

INTRODUCTION

We all need space. Space to think, space to breathe, space to go wild and space to curl up. We need space where we can dream and think about the future and we need space to discuss what's going on right here and now. We also need space for *our* shoes and *their* toys. This book is about how to create that space. Not storage space exactly but the space you need in order to be all the roles you've acquired in your life – Lover, Mother, Daughter, Wife. Creating the right space and designing a calm home is more than interior design or even architecture. Your home needs to be designed to support you and love you the way you support and love it. You need to design your home with more than your average design tools – beyond the designer labels, the eye-wateringly expensive items and the fashionistas opinion. Yes, of course we want our homes to look gorgeous, let's take that as a given, but on top of that we need to design happiness and sanity into our homes.

But how do we purposefully design a home that is happy? Doesn't that depend on what your version of happy is? Is happy a Home Sweet Home sampler or is it simply somewhere you can shut the door behind you and escape? What is your definition of a happy home? A place of comfort and strength for you and your family, a party pad, a sanctuary, your castle, perhaps? However you define home, don't you want somewhere you are genuinely proud of, somewhere you feel confident inviting friends and family to, somewhere that is 'just so you'? Perhaps your home is already like that, in which case, congratulations and let's just add some decorative touches, or maybe you've got some more fundamental work to do.

Wouldn't you like to create spaces that are:

1. Designed around your personal needs (rather than those of the architect from the last century who designed it)?
2. Organised in a way that suits you (how you work, how your kids live and play, how you spend your time with others)?
3. Decorated in a style that actually reflects what you want to say about yourself to the world (I'm discrete and elegant, I'm loud and bubbly, I'm glamorous and attention seeking...)?

Who am I?

My name is Niki Schäfer and I'm an interior designer and a lifestyle coach. I help busy women, mums and house-lovers create their own home style. I teach them how to make the most of their space and manage the process of re-design (without losing the plot or accidentally divorcing a husband) so they can create a place that loves them (as much as they love it).

I've designed a system called 'Dwell-Being', which I'm going to take you through in this book. This system will help you create an environment that truly reflects who you are and want to be. Together we'll design a space that will not only look fabulous it will also organise your beautiful (but ridiculously busy) life and genuinely meet your needs. The impact of this is that life will become simpler, it means less hassle, more comfort, combined with a sense of stability and protection, which in turn means that everyone will feel better there. People will live more collaboratively (... they might even get on together!)

I see myself as part designer, part investigator, part psychologist, part storyteller, part artist and I major in communication. This book and the Dwell-Being system is a combination of these parts. I hope you enjoy it. I hope it helps. (I hope you will write and let me know where there are improvements to be made so I can pass on your message too. niki@dwell-being.co.uk)

Home truths

But before we get too excited let's start with a few questions... a few 'home truths'.

- Have you ever put off doing anything to the house because you won't be living there for long and then think the same again more than 5 years later?
- Have you ever thought there's no point in making the house look nice while there are young kids running around trashing the place?
- Have you ever watched days and days of interior design programmes and then done exactly nothing at all about making any improvements on your own home?

- Have you ever resented, been frustrated, bored to tears or just mind-numbingly exhausted by how much time you spend looking after the house?
- Have you ever decorated a room only to sit back and realise you've played everything completely safe and now your room is beyond dull?
- Have you ever had taste clashes with your husband that have ended in a, let's call it, 'heated debate'?
- Have you ever been concerned about what other people think of your home and thought people judge *you* based on what your house looks like?
- Have you ever wondered how to stop the whinging and moaning in your home and wished everyone had some of their own space?
- Have you ever wanted a bedroom where you can truly relax and have magnificent sex with your husband (this programme does not in any way guarantee the latter...) in a space created just for you?
- Have you ever wondered how you would feel about your home if you'd designed it to suit what is really going on in your life and decorated it so it really suited you?

Dwell-Being

Home-life is always changing, kids don't stand still, they grow up and yes, they'll be off to University before we know it, or maybe they'll be living upstairs until they're in their mid-forties desperately looking for a house of their own. It doesn't matter, the point is that for now, and for the foreseeable future, we want harmony and an environment that is going to do the best for everyone concerned. Don't we?

I have lived in more than 100 places (I was brought up in the RAF and later became a bit of a globetrotter) and have seen many different styles, shapes and sizes of somewhere called 'home'. However, I didn't really think about it from my own perspective until I had a family of my own (I have three children aged four, seven and ten) and wanted to create roots. I wanted a home of my own. This is what I wanted:

I no longer wanted to be moving every few years, I wanted some stability for the kids (and honestly, the school choices are just too mind-boggling to be changing too often). I wanted a home that looked great but didn't consume all my waking hours to get it looking like that. I like to throw a decent dinner together for my family and friends but I don't need a celebrity chef kitchen, just somewhere that suits how I work. I wanted a place where I could do my own stuff without being invaded by the squeaks and squeals of children's TV and yet I wanted a space that was open enough for me to keep an eye on what they're all up to. I wanted some private space and some public space - some places to show off and others where no one would ever see. I wanted a place that supported me and my ever-evolving family's needs but most of all, I wanted us all to be happy there. And sane.

How do you create a happy home? I asked. (We'll get on to sane later).

Creating a happy home

No one seemed to have a straight answer. There were snippets here and clues there but nothing concrete, no system to follow, no step-by-step guide and so I set off in search of my own solutions.

I visited the world of interior decoration where they know how to make a room beautiful. I learnt from interior designers how to sculpt space to become functional and efficient and equally brimming with emotion - be it nostalgia, passion, excitement or drama. I borrowed a few tricks and techniques from a world I used to work in - the advertising industry - where creativity is balanced with commerce, where creating brands is based on the principles of friendship - encouraging trust, reliability and loyalty and I then delved head first into the personal development and life-coaching worlds where happiness strategies are formulated and relationships are key. And then I set about merging these worlds. Balancing them, at times one atop another, other times starting completely from scratch.

I became a bit of a balancing act as a result – some elements in perfect equilibrium, others more a circus act. My roots are from Yorkshire but at times my thinking has a distinctively Californian twang. My day job is designing fabulous rooms yet my relaxation is kickboxing and neuroscience. I focus on space but I love people the most. I studied hard to be balanced.

When I started on this path, I was exhausted, to say the least. I was a mother covered in baby sick, with a muffin-top belly and a non-existent social life. I was blessed to have an incredibly supportive husband but I'm afraid I didn't treat him as well as he did me. The boredom of looking after the house and the endless chores and mundane day-in-day-out schedule of looking after kids did not suit me and I would remind him about this. Daily.

It took him 12 months to persuade me to do something for me. How could this possibly be the answer? I asked him. (Desperately wanting it to be the answer, yet still riddled with guilt that I could actually get something out of the situation for me.) But he persuaded me to study and the impact of that has been immeasurable. Because once you start to study where do you stop?

I'm not talking about Chemistry A-level here. I'm talking about studying myself. Taking the time to find subjects that interest me. Just taking the time to focus on myself. The ramifications of this alone have been enormous.

What time do you take for yourself?

Do you take any at all? When was the last time you thought about what you are doing? Or are you simply on auto-pilot? Are you just flogging the same old territory hoping that something will change? Are you making the same mistakes? Do you even think they're mistakes? Are they just the 'I've got to's and the 'I'm supposed to's that have kept you going so far?

But are these 'duties' bringing about the results you've actually been hoping for? Is your home what you want it to be? Is your life heading in the direction you want it to be going in? If you carried on the way you're going now, where will you be in five years' time? Where in 10? Is that the place you want to be in, in 10 years' time? It's a question worth thinking about. But more so, where would you be if you made a few simple changes today? Where would you be if you created an environment that truly supported your visions and your goals, that reflected your views of the world and that cared for your family's health and your own sanity? Where would that trajectory take you?

Today, while my belly isn't perfectly flat, my muffin-top has gone. The baby sick has thankfully gone too and I have more energy than almost anyone I know. My social life isn't what it was in my 20s but then again I don't want it to be. Instead I fill my time doing what truly pleases me - painting, writing, indulging in weird and wonderful therapies and workshops with really interesting people, designing homes, coaching clients, speaking publicly, kickboxing, walking, studying neuroscience, swimming, gardening, arranging parties, traveling, the occasional massage and talking. I love to talk.

My home does not look like there's an interior designer living here and I'm pleased about that. I want my home to feel lived in. I want people to come here and relax, to come and kick off their shoes and perch on the sofa arm with a glass in their hand and a smile on their face. I do not want people nervous about dirtying the carpet or smudging the highly polished furniture (which is why I have neither...). My home is where I want to entertain. It's where I comfort my kids after a bad day at school or where I celebrate their achievements. It's where we have pancakes and practice karate. It's where family comes for Christmas and was even where my daughter was born (it wasn't planned.... long story!). My home is, as clichéd as it sounds, very much where my heart is and while I yearn for a Huf Haus overlooking the crashing waves, I know that my home today is just what I need right now.

It's worth thinking about: what do you need in your home today?

Why do we need Dwell-Being now?
Part I - the power of transformation

Much like yourself, I'm sure, Gok Wan, Trinny and Susannah, DIY SOS and Changing Rooms have been part of my life for years and while it is entertaining to see people walking down the catwalk in the nude and watching Laurence Llewellyn Bowen's fabulous showmanship, I have found the psychological transformations of the people involved are the most addictive part of the show. Time and time again, I've seen people transformed - their character, their attitude, their approach to life – not because of years of psychiatric and psychological help but because someone has shown them how to make the most of themselves - with something as 'superficial' as fashion or a new decor. Outstanding.

This is a talent we truly need in today's living. The ability to make people feel good about who they truly are.

The transformations are also evident in the likes of Changing Rooms and most certainly in DIY SOS, where whole families are given the kiss of life by the completion of an extension, a kitchen and an attic room conversion. It's powerful stuff.

On the other hand, I'm equally rather frustrated with the interior design TV shows because they give a very false impression of firstly how long it takes to refurbish (60 minutes... give me a break) and also they don't show the process of how designs are chosen for specific people (or whether or not their tastes and needs have even been taken into consideration).

My conclusion has been that there's a real need to explain how design actually works, as opposed to just showing the - albeit very realistic - drama of designers screaming and electricians moaning. And more specifically how to choose something that will work for you, as opposed to the family on the telly, who don't have the same needs, style or budget as you (because the programme-maker covered their costs).

Why do we need Dwell-Being now?
Part II - the relief a system can bring

I have worked in many offices, some corporate and swanky and others a great deal less so. However, on my first day, I have always been shown how to alter my chair and adjust my computer screen so my head and my body are in the correct position. During the first week of most jobs, there has been an induction session that can be painfully long or somewhat inadequate, but it has always existed. A guided tour has been provided, key people have been introduced, systems have been explained, manuals handed out and training sessions have been dutifully scheduled for the weeks to come. This should be a familiar tale to anyone who has ever worked in a corporate environment.

But why is there no such practice for a home? Are there practitioners of well-being for the home who will adjust our proverbial office chair? Are there best practice manuals on how to create an environment that will bring out the finest in our family? Are there industry wide codes and systems that will bring efficiency and organisation to a house of three, four or five inhabitants? Are there even some rules of thumb? They were not given to me. Did I miss that memo? Or that tweet?

I think it wise to point out early on that a home can never be standardised and mechanised to a factory setting. Who would want to live there? Robots perhaps, C3PO, K-9 and the likes, not you and me. However, I do believe that a guiding hand would be well worth its weight in gold.

And so I have designed a book that will guide you through a process of transformation - not only of your home but also of your family life. It will take you by the hand and show you how to create the home you deserve.

11

"Happiness is not an accident, nor is it something you wish for, happiness is something you design."
Jim Rohn

How to use the Dwell-Being system

There are three foundations to a home:
- The art of personal style
- The science of family thinking
- The discipline of house rules

This book will help you build these foundations by guiding you through the Dwell-Being design process – a journey through the seven spaces of your home.

- Outer Space
- Me Space
- Head Space
- Thinking Space
- Dream Space
- Breathing Space
- Heart Space

Each of these spaces represent an area in your house and an aspect of your life. Designing them (as opposed to just putting up with what's there) will help you make the best use of the space and create a calm, sane and outrageously gorgeous home.

DWELL-BEING MODEL

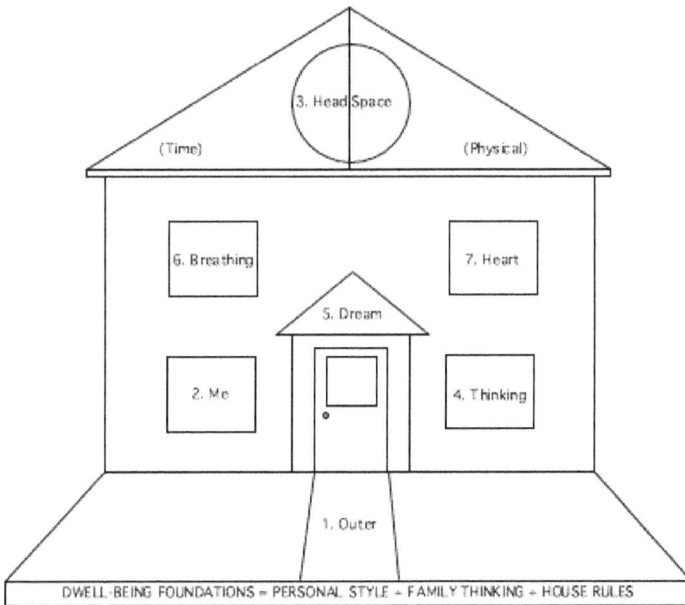

There are a number of exercises and tools, as well as stories and theory, that will guide you through the process and by the end you will have a firm idea of how to design your own home (and keep everyone in it relatively sane). You will know how to plan spaces that match your activities - both the body's activities but equally as importantly, the activities of the brain.

This book is based on both the aesthetics of interior design – the art - and also on practical psychology – the science, or to be more precise, the neuroscience. How we think is fundamental to our happiness and this guide will show you how to adapt your current thinking into something that will honestly benefit you and your family. And if you really pay attention to the neuroscience (and by that I mean do the homework and exercises in the book) you'll suddenly start to see positive shifts happening throughout your life – in and out of the home. (This can be quite a surreal experience because, beyond the exercises, it really takes no other effort on your behalf. If you change your thinking, things around you will start to change too. Don't say I haven't warned you...)

The seven spaces of Dwell-Being

This is what you can expect to learn from the seven chapters:

FOUNDATION 1: PERSONAL STYLE

Outer Space
o   Home values - discover your personal meaning of home.
o   Home approach – understand the power of first impressions.

Me Space
o   Dwell-Being concept board - conceive a 'signature style' for your own home.

Head Space
o   Personal space - understand the importance of space for yourself.
o   Time design - find space and time to think.

FOUNDATION 2: FAMILY THINKING

Thinking Space
o House dynamics - coordinate your thinking style with the patterns and styles of the rest of the family.

Dream Space
o Sleeping spaces - design places to sleep.
o Goal design - make space to envision life as you want it.

Breathing Space
o Chill out zones - craft places to relax.
o The science of being - establish space to connect with your family and friends and to just 'be'.

Heart Space
o Heart of the home - organise places to eat and be together.
o Heartfelt communication - build space to feel, to listen, and to be heard.

FOUNDATION 3: HOUSE RULES

Conclusion
o Housekeeping
o House rules - dos and don'ts.

The Dwell-Being system

There are four different zones to each space - home truths, picture house, insider secrets and homework. These zones work together to create the Dwell-Being system. They don't follow on sequentially from each other, like a formula, but work harmoniously together to create a cohesive effect. (Much like all the parts of a room work together to create a cohesive decorative scheme - the lights showing off the sculpture, the colours working in harmony, the patterns repeated rhythmically throughout the room). Each zone has been designed to help you build confidence, understanding and the skills required to create a home you can be proud of. This means that you can rely on the Dwell-Being system working in the background while you simply enjoy the journey through your home.

Zones

Home Truths
This is 'telling it like it is'. It's what we (mums and busy women) face every day. Home truths are also Dwell-Being thoughts in a nutshell.

Picture House
These are the images and drawings in the book. A picture is worth a thousand words so you'll be able to see what I'm talking about here.

Insider Secrets
These are the parables, quotes and tips that feature in every space. You'll also find real life examples of work I have done with clients in the case studies. Often we learn so much more through a story (or a bit of insider gossip)

Homework

There will be hard-core exercises for those who love the drill and really want to make the most of this book.
There will be easy-come easy-go suggestions for those who hate being told what to do.

Thanks

It seems as good a place as any to thank those from whom I have borrowed, stolen and simply learnt. My teachers are many and I encourage you to investigate and learn from any of the names you recognise and look up any you don't. (My mum's name is in here though... just to warn you.)

The personal development, achievement, thinking and feeling crowd: Tony Robbins, Joseph McClendon III, Brendon Burchard, Steve Covey, Brian Tracy, Frank Kern, Eben Pagan, Jamie Smart, Marie Forleo, Jim Rohn, Brene Brown, Byron Katie, Jay Abraham, Jay Niblick, Jonathan Haidt, Richard Bandler, Tad James, Napoleon Hill, Derren Brown, Malcolm Gladwell, Sam Gosling, Robert Cialdini, John Carlton, Sir Ken Robinson, Sage Robbins, Michael Gerber, David Shephard, Ewan Mochrie, Jenni Smallshaw, Nikki Warnes, Jorgen and Davina Rasmussen, Luke Dorn, Rachel and Richie McHale, Laurelle Rond, Dr Lynda Shaw, Amber Kelly, Sally Webb, Sylvia Baldock, Vicky Heriot, Alison Pressley and Denise O'Dwyer.

My working world: APL, GGT, Leagas Delaney, Berlin Cameron, Unilever, Nestle Rowntree, Nintendo, Studio

Editions, Sara Bennison, Jane Geraghty, Tim Browne, Addison James, Richard Armstrong, Malcolm White, Steve Zaroff, Laura Stevens, Kim Manzi, Michael Vesey, Laurence Blume, Andrew Powell, and Nick Chapin.

The design world: KLC School of Design, Chelsea College of Art and Design, TVU, Diana McKnight, Lyndall Fernie, Kevin McCloud, George Clarke, Jamie Anley, Naomi Cleaver, Laurence Llewellyn Bowen, Gok Wan and many more..

The most important lot: Richard Schäfer, Genna, Finn and Zoe Grace, Steve and Barbara Cartwright, Jill Cartwright, Ali Poulton, UPiW and Valerie Upton, Kenneth and Isabel Nicholls, Mary and Frank Cartwright, Walter and Angela Schäfer, Naomi Tegg and Mel Robinson.

To you all, I am truly grateful. Now let's begin.

FOUNDATION 1
PERSONAL STYLE

Space 1 – Outer Space

"He is happiest, be he king or peasant, who finds peace in his home."
Johann Wolfgang von Goethe

DWELL-BEING MODEL

DWELL-BEING FOUNDATIONS – PERSONAL STYLE – FAMILY THINKING – HOUSE RULES

There are seven distinct spaces in a house. It is both an art and a science getting each space right. The Dwell-Being system is a simple journey through these spaces, designed for you to build a genuine understanding and clear ideas about what will make your home calm, sane and outrageously gorgeous. Dwell-Being is about balance – creating structure as well as beauty, designing a house that feels good as well as looks good.

These are the steps of the journey you have ahead and what you can expect from them.

FOUNDATION 1: PERSONAL STYLE

Outer Space
o   Now you're going to discover the meaning of home and the importance of first impressions.
o   And learn how to carve out a safe space from the outside world.

Me Space
o   Dwell-Being concept board - conceive a 'signature style' for your own home.

Head Space
o   Find a space for yourself.
o   Carve out the time to design your dream home.
o   Understand how to control your roles in the home.

FOUNDATION 2: FAMILY THINKING

Thinking Space
o   House dynamics - coordinate your thinking style with the patterns and styles of the rest of the family.

Dream Space
o   Sleeping spaces - design places to sleep.
o   Goal design - make space to envision life as you want it.

Breathing Space
o   Chill out zones - craft places to relax.
The science of being - establish space to connect with family and friends to just 'be'.

Heart Space
o   Heart of the home - organise places to eat and be together.
o   Heartfelt communication - build space to feel, to listen, to be heard and to be loved.

FOUNDATION 3: HOUSE RULES

Conclusion
o   Establish house rules - dos and don'ts
o   Housekeeping - feel confident in your understanding and your skills.

Outer space chapter outcomes

• Know where you belong.

- Understand how our basic human needs are met by our home.
- Work out what your property has to offer and how to make the most of it.
- Feel a deep sense of fulfilment whenever you walk through your front door (assuming it's the right front door into the right home...)

Home truth

It's all very well wishing to design our dream home but if we don't have a clear idea of what *home* actually means, then how are we going to go about it? The 'home truth' is that we frequently set off to accomplish something, we're determined and we're ambitious, but if stopped to ask where we are going or, more to the point, what we are really hoping to achieve, we are often brought to a grinding halt. We simply don't know.

Success

One of the fundamental lessons in 'how to succeed' (as broad a topic you'll be hard pressed to find) is to be very clear about what it is that you want to achieve. In the next chapter – Me Space - we will investigate the look and feel of the home you want to achieve. This will help you work out the aesthetics and the decoration but this book is also about discovering the meaning of your home because, while beauty is part of what creates well-being and happiness, there are many other facets besides.

Homes can be so much more than magnolia coloured walls and a three-piece suite from the 80s. Home has the power to be meaningful. It can give you a sense of security and comfort one minute but then excitement or efficiency or simply happiness the next. Let's discover what you want your home to mean to you.

What does your home mean to you?

How would you describe the concept of 'home' to an alien? (I ask you purely on the basis that this chapter is called Outer Space). What would you tell the intergalactic visitor? What is the first thing you would say about the home? Would you describe it in terms of protection and security, as a source of heat and shelter? Or would you leap into more psychological aspects of what the home provides to us humans?

Would it make sense to our green and googly-eyed friend to group ourselves into small units (houses) and create a small domain (fenced garden) around us? Would you be able to explain the choice of materials and the layout of the house – why a terraced house for example, over a log cabin? And then, how would you go about explaining the need to beautify the space? Isn't a strong fence, a good fire and comfy bed enough? Why do you think we have come to take such pleasure from the home? And could you explain this to the alien or would he return to his communal living arrangement on board the utilitarian and purely functional spaceship thinking you a little 'emotional'?

How your home helps to meet your needs

Your house is an incredibly important part of your life. It is the stage on which a great deal of your 'story' is played out. As a result, I believe it should be designed to meet as many of your needs as possible. If many of your needs (basic and complex) are met by your home – something that surrounds you and is somewhere that you return to on a (probably) daily basis - then doesn't it make sense that your home should support you to move forward and make the most of your life? Let's examine this a little deeper.

What are our needs and how do they relate to the home? It's not often we sit and think about our basic human needs, (we have a tendency to take them for granted and watch the TV instead). The world of psychology has been endeavouring to understand our needs and how to meet them for hundreds of years. I have borrowed from that world and used the psychologist Abraham Maslow's famous hierarchy of needs to gain an understanding of what motivates us.

What needs do we seek to meet first? And how do these relate to the home?

Maslow's famous hierarchy of needs

- Basic needs
- Safety needs
- Belonging needs
- Esteem needs
- Cognitive needs

- Aesthetic needs
- Self-actualisation
- Transcendence

These terms may seem a little academic but that is generally the way with psychology, and it certainly was in 1943 when they were written. We will expand on them as we go along, starting with my basic interpretation of how I believe they relate to the home.

The Dwell-Being hierarchy of needs

- Basic needs – somewhere warm, where you can sleep, eat and drink.
- Safety needs – a place to feel secure and certain that our life has meaning.
- Belongingness and love needs – a place to love and be loved and to accept others.
- Esteem – a place to express our accomplishments and status.
- Cognitive needs – a place to learn and gain a better understanding of the world.
- Aesthetic needs – the presence of beauty, art and nature, which leads to a feeling of oneness.
- Self-actualisation – to help us become everything we want to be.
- Transcendence – helping others self-actualise.

Maslow stated that as we fulfil each need, we go on to seek the next level. We find somewhere warm and safe before we think about its aesthetics. We seek love and a sense of belonging before we seek to learn. And we progress up this pyramid until we reach 'self-actualisation' and ultimately 'transcendence'. These words do not have very concrete interpretations, and can seem deliberately vague in their meaning. This is probably because they are entirely personal and therefore unique to each person. However, these are my interpretations.

Self-actualisation is when you become the *real* you, the authentic you, the true you. To paraphrase Maslow:

"What a woman can be, she must be."

Transcendence literally means 'going beyond', which I take to mean going *beyond* my real self. To where? A personal destination.

(It might be worth pointing out that the personal destination isn't likely to be Magaluf or the beaches of Ibiza, but then again you could think otherwise. Let's get back to Maslow.)

Can you see where you fit within the hierarchy and which needs you are currently trying to fulfil through your home? Obviously you don't get a badge to sew on to your sleeve with each level but if you consider the needs, it's fair to say that one might lead to the next. Maslow's needs are often depicted using a pyramid shape and again this has meaning, because the solidity and grounding of the basic needs layers are required before moving up to the more esoteric levels above. Appreciating beauty is one thing but does it keep you warm? Self-actualisation and even transcendence are admirable targets but if you don't have a solid esteem to base them on, they are unlikely to give you ultimate peace of mind.

How does your home currently meet your needs?

1. Basic needs

Are you in the luxurious position of being able to use and appreciate the house as somewhere to sleep, eat and drink? Or are you still in a caravan envying the builders their freedom of space in your house (even if they are filthy and probably freezing cold)?

2. Safety needs

Is your domain secure? Do you feel safe as you lock the door at night and go to bed? Are the walls that surround you there to protect you? Do you feel the comfort of that protection?

And how about the much larger question: Does your home and the security it provides give you a sense of meaning to your life? Do you feel an accomplishment for owning a property and for providing security for you and your family?

3. Belongingness and love needs

Do you feel a real emotional love towards your home? Do you see it as somewhere you are loved and you love others? Is it a place of acceptance (or just grinning and bearing it)?

4. Esteem needs

Are you proud of your home? Are there items on display that bring about comments of admiration from others? Is the house itself a statement piece? Do you feel your home matches how you feel about your status in life? Or has this thought never even crossed your mind?

5. Cognitive needs

I don't think you need to own a library to meet this need, however, do you feel that your home is a place where you can learn and grow? Does your home help you gain a better understanding of the world around you?

6. Aesthetic needs

Does your home look beautiful? To you. The expression about beauty being in the eye of the beholder is incredibly important. It doesn't matter at all what your next-door neighbour, the postman, or even your mother-in-law believe. It's about what you think of it. The effect is on you. Is there beauty, art or an enjoyment of nature in your home that you feel contributes to the sense of your home, and to your well-being and happiness?

7. Self-actualisation needs

The solid foundations of your home can give you support and comfort, but does your home also give you the power to be able to recognise who you truly are? We will look into this in greater depth in the 'Me Space' chapter but it's worth thinking about now. How much of you is reflected in your home? And is it the 'you' you want to see staring back at you every day?

8. Transcendence

How does your home contribute to helping others reach their full potential? It is important to note that you must come first in this. (I will labour this point – about the importance of you – later, so be warned). Once YOU have reached self-actualisation, how do your surroundings help you to help others do the same?

"And how on earth can a pile of bricks and mortar do all this?" you might well be asking.

Property emotions

How did you go about buying your home? Can you remember? Was it purely a logical decision based on school locations and property value? Or was there an emotional element to it? Because while school proximity is vital (as are your financial arrangements, obviously) the emotional side of the house plays an equally important role in how you end up living there on a day-to-day basis. Let's look at the aspects of a house that will bring out the 'warm and fuzzy' in you. (This will be particularly helpful if you are in the sometimes frustrating and very often time-consuming phase of looking to buy a new home.)

Architectural style

You may have a predilection for a certain type of home. A red brick box built in the 70s might be your idea of a horror or you might think it a hassle-free family pad for a few years (even if you end up living there for decades.) You may have a view on whether a cottage is right for you and your family (and need no understanding of the principles of architecture to do so). You might envy the proportions of a Georgian façade but feel it a little grand for your own home. You could see the Victorian mansion with eyes that value solidity and sturdiness, or perhaps you seek something a little lighter and more contemporary. A modern, flat-roof white box with huge panels of glass could appeal to one type of person but remind another of a fridge or a goldfish bowl. We have very emotional reactions to homes, for sure.

Context

How the house fits into the surrounding area will also play a role in how you perceive it. It could be the grandest, most ostentatious of buildings but, if it's in the middle of a housing estate, it's not going to feel the same as it would up on a hillside with magnificent views. Standing out from the crowd most certainly has its place but being a sore thumb is not the way to do this. Understanding the community and the building's context is a very emotional aspect of choosing a home, for these are the people who will be your neighbours and hopefully ultimately, your friends. Do their homes and their lives look like the homes and lives you would like to be involved in?

Niki Schäfer

Orientation

Whether you are aware of it directly or not, the way a house is oriented will have an impression on you. This is something that requires great thought when you are in the luxurious position of owning a plot and working out where to build the house. The view from the house will be key in this decision but so too is the view from the road when seeing the house for the first time. Do you want to see it square on? Or do a curve and a sense of intrigue add to the interest of the house?

Natural light

The orientation of the building will also dictate the light available to the house. Being trapped behind the monolith that is the next-door house will certainly have an impact on you. Who wants to be living in the shadow of someone else? Who wants to be watched over from another house? Who wants to be able to see into next-door's bedroom windows? Horrible.

A home with ample light will have a very beneficial psychological effect on the people who live there. Light is something we humans are naturally attracted to (we walk towards it quite unconsciously as we enter a room) and making the most of it is a fundamental part of the design success. When you looked around your home for the first time, you will have discussed the lightness of each room without a doubt, whether you are a design professional or not. It's simply something we need, physically and emotionally.

Amenities

Without wanting to sound like an estate agent's brochure, it's important to note how close the 'resources' are to our home. In the past (before the days of Internet grocery shopping) we would have looked for water, wood, a source of food (fish, deer etc.) and a sense of protection from the elements, but equally a space where we're not trapped. These requirements still play a role in our psyche. And while water comes from a tap, heat arrives at the touch of a button and food can be delivered in a matter of minutes, we still have an innate sense of whether our environment is good for us.

Obstacles

We can certainly tell when the environment is wrong for us. The electricity pylon at the end of the road is not going to appeal. The river that floods on an annual basis is going to have its downsides. The busy road at the front of the house is going to be a concern for both noise and young children. The planning permission for a fish and chip shop next door will cause olfactory decision-making skills to kick in. Sometimes we can't even put our finger on why it is we dislike a place. Of course, this drives sellers and estate agents insane but the gut feel of a home is very powerful and if it's wrong, there's nothing you can do to change that. Go with your gut every time.

Memories

This is purely emotion. The seemingly illogical bias involved in admiring a house that reminds you of a happy family holiday or rejecting another because it triggers feelings of a school friend whose father was mean to you doesn't matter to anyone else but you. If you don't like it for whatever reason, you don't like it! Of course, over time, you will create new memories for the house if you stay there, but if your memories are powerful in the first place it is worth paying attention to them and not buying the house (assuming they are negative). If they are positive then simply be aware of the emotional wave you are riding and still consider all the practical aspects of the house too. It may well look like the house from Little House on the Prairie, a programme you adored as a child and the kind you have always wanted to live in but remember the school run is 20 minutes each way and the only pub in the village serves a bad pint.

Case study

During the renovation of the stairwell in Paul and Janine's home, we were discussing a small and obscure space in the wall that had been created by a badly designed stair in front of a wall. Our immediate thought was to close this hole up but I suddenly remembered being a child and sitting on the staircase waiting for my Dad to come home from work. I asked whether their kids did the same and Paul laughed as I mentioned it. Wouldn't it be a shame to lose this little cubby-hole view for the kids? I asked.

It's important to remember that the homes we provide for our kids are what they will believe 'home' means.

Little irregularities, special nooks and crannies are the characteristics that will stay with a child far longer than the removable stickers that plaster the wall so transiently. A treasured window seat or an odd shaped window is a far more powerful representation of home in a future memory.

What nooks and crannies do you remember from your childhood houses that still mean 'home' to you?

Houses are, without a doubt, emotional. And no wonder, for after all, they are the stage for our life stories. Understanding what impact they have on us and then learning to harness the effects to our benefit is what this book is about. So let's start at the beginning by looking at the front of the home and seeing what we can do about it.

Homework – human and property needs

Go through the human needs and the property emotions and see how you and your house feel to one another. This is an 'awareness' exercise that will help you later on. It is important to make note of how you feel now so that you can look back later and see how much progress has been made. And while this might not be of multiple-choice simplicity, it's worthwhile giving the answers some thought and then writing a quick sentence or two for each of the categories:

- Basic needs – does your home keep you warm?
- Safety needs – do you feel secure in your home?

- Belongingness and love needs – do you feel like you belong in your home?
- Esteem needs – does your home reflect what you want to say about you?
- Cognitive needs – do you learn through your home?
- Aesthetic needs – is your home beautiful?
- Self-actualisation needs – can you be you (the real you) in your home?
- Transcendence needs – does your environment help you help others to become the *real* them?
- Architectural style – is it your cup of tea?
- Context – what's the neighbourhood like?
- Orientation – what are the views like?
- Natural light – is there plenty or are you in the dark?
- Amenities – what facilities do you have nearby?
- Obstacles – are there dangers or eye-sores?
- Memories – what roles are your memories playing?

First impressions count

Kerb appeal is one of the most important aspects of your home. 'House doctors' and estate agents understand the value of making a good first impression. Much like that first handshake in a job interview, people have made up their minds long before you start to talk about your finer qualities and equally, people (the Tesco delivery man, the Jehovah's witness or your best friend) will make a judgement about your home based on what the front area looks like.

Your home's impressions

It's not a bad idea to think about the run up to your home. How does it look to you? Is that different from how it looks to others? You might be of the opinion that what other people think doesn't matter. "Let them think what they like!" you say. And there's nothing wrong with this. However, it is worth bearing in mind that the 'impression' is being made not only to people who see the place with fresh eyes, for the first time, but it is also having a much deeper impression on those who see it day-in-day-out.

Habits are built on repetitive thinking (not repetitive action as you might have believed) therefore it is incredibly important to keep our thoughts as 'healthy' as possible. Because, whether your thoughts are positive or negative, there are long-term consequences. Let's think about it with something completely irrelevant so you can see it and understand it easily from another perspective.

Pushing fashion

Do you remember when pedal pushers came out in the 80s? I should imagine that your first question would have been the same as mine at the time: "Why has someone put on those ridiculous trousers?" You turn to your friend and say as much and she replies, "Because they are in fashion". "What?" you ask in reply, barely able to contain your incredulity. The week rolls by and you see another pair of the ridiculous trousers on a woman who in every other respect looks very together and fashionable. And then again on another women who also seems quite normal. You start to waver. An open magazine spread reveals another pair of the pedal pushers in question, this time on a famous person and you take one step closer to believing your friend is actually right.

A month later you walk into town and meet your friend and lo and behold you see that she too is wearing the garment. You smile and compliment her on her fashionable choice. You see them in the shops and you stop and admire them. You walk into the shop, try on the pedal pushers, admire yourself and then buy them with your saved up pocket money. You walk into the street swinging your high street fashion bag, containing super on trend pedal pushers and you feel good about the world.

(Please note that this may or may not be based on a true story and any likeness to the author's childhood fashion finding is purely coincidental and not the point of the story.)

It was all a case of thinking. It was the thinking that led to such a fashion statement. A mere month or so beforehand, the idea of pedal pushers was laughable but a round of 'altered thinking' about the item slowly but surely brought with it a whole new belief system.

Now while I use a light-hearted example here to show you how easy it is for us to change opinion and form a completely new one, the truth is that this is what happens to us with all our thoughts. And that's a thought worth thinking about.

It's like a playground rumour. How quickly can you start one? How quickly can something that's actually made up become gospel truth? The exact same process works in your head with thoughts that are useful and equally with thoughts that are very harmful. The more you talk them over, the more you consider them, the more you ponder, the more you share them with others, the more you own them, the more convinced you will become.

If you are coming home every day and badmouthing (outwardly or just in thought) your home, what effect do you think this is having? You may well think it's just a fleeting thought, it's normal to have a bit of a moan, even in your head, but it's important to note that these thoughts are slowly becoming much stronger. You are convincing yourself.

Conviction

What would you rather be convinced about? What beliefs do you think would be healthier for you to adopt? I'm sure you can think of plenty, but let's start with our thoughts about the home. What do you want to believe about the home?

Personally I would like to believe it is a source of both comfort and strength. I think it should cheer me up, protect me, excite me in some spaces and calm me in others. I want to show off some rooms, yet keep others purely to myself. I think efficiency is critical in some areas and not so important in others. I want interesting things to look at, pictures or objects that remind me of somewhere or make me momentarily reflective but equally I don't want the house turning into a memory museum. I want it to be fun, light-hearted, maybe even enough to crack a smile. A home has to be flexible it seems, but one thing I want for sure is to be able to walk through my front door and be able to shut away the rest of the world.

The right impression

Wouldn't it be a powerful idea to be able to use the front door as a reminder, a trigger that I am leaving one head space (we'll be discussing these at length in a couple of chapters) and entering another?

What would your front door have to look like to remind you to shift your thinking? I believe this is far more important than what your front door looks like, of course, but let's start there and see if we can work our way through the rest of the house, clearing up the thinking and making sure the idea of home, what it looks and like and ultimately what it means to you and your children, is how you want to perceive and believe in it.

A tour of your home

Imagine yourself walking down the street towards home or just driving round the corner into your street. You have that sensation of being 'nearly there'. Your mind clicks into 'getting inside' mode and you pull into the drive or walk up the path to your door. Which door do you go in? The front door or the side entrance? Which is the door that feels most welcoming to you?

You walk to the door and start the familiar rummage in your handbag for the house keys. You may well have a number of other items in your arms, it won't be unheard of if you have a baby car seat, plus child, in there too. You finally find the key rings and feel the weight of the familiar keys (and all the aspects of your life they open too). I would like to suggest to you that among these keys you see a fob – something that will spell home to you, it could be a tassel, it could be a heart, it could be a miniature figure of Laurence Llewellyn Bowen, whatever you choose, but look at the fob and recognise that it embodies the feelings you want to have for your home. And it makes you smile. You smile as you put the key in the door and as you pull or turn the door handle you can feel the power and magic of home.

You open the door and turn on the lights. The space warms up immediately and welcomes you. A painting on the wall is highlighted and you smile at the memory of buying it with your husband on holiday. You open the cupboards to put away your coat and the paint colour in there still surprises you. You love this little space, how tidy and efficient it has become since you decorated it and bought some fun hooks for the kids to use properly. You walk into the kitchen and feel the now familiar sense of organisation and yet homeliness that has been evident since you designed it to work the way you cook in it. You pick up a child's drawing and put it back on the fridge where it belongs with the rest of the week's artwork and you smile.

You head to the living room and turn on the lights but instead of the bright down-lights that used to burst into action you now have a small number of lights dotted around the room that create areas of interest. A reading light by an armchair, a picture light over a piece of art your Grandfather left you, an uplighter that picks out the detailing in the textured wallpaper you still adore. Thank goodness you decided to be brave and not just go for paint on that wall.

You head upstairs to change your shoes and as you walk up the staircase you go through the stories that each photo brings with it - the family portrait makes you laugh as you remember the day, the pictures of the children when they were very young makes you remember how little they still are really, the picture of you as a teenager reminds you that you too are still young, you still feel like the girl in the photo.

You enter your bedroom and turn on the light. The bed head fabric looks so beautiful and the throw and cushions pick out the colour you've always loved in the picture frames that sit on both bedside tables. You stroke the bed throw as you sit next to it and take a nice deep breath. You smile inside as you feel the environment around you whisper quietly in your ear that you are safe, you are home.

Home assessment homework – part 1

Do you feel good at the thought of this kind of tour of your home or are you still stumped with incredulity of having such a source of comfort and strength at your disposal? Was the Laurence Llewellyn Bowen key ring fob just too much for you? Let's break this story down again and have a look at some of the feel good factors. Your homework (part one) is simply to become aware of each of these aspects of your home. Part two involves doing something about it!

1. Home approach

How do you feel as you approach your home? Over the next week stop just before you put the key in the latch and assess how you feel. Are you relieved? Are you intimidated by the amount of work there is to do on the other side? Do you feel you've reached a safe and secure place? Are you excited?

Decide how you would like to feel instead. Once you have become aware of a feeling, it becomes much easier to control, so after a few days of simply pausing at the front door and scanning yourself for your feelings, you could start inserting the feeling that you actually want to feel. Why not put something at the front door to remind you to do this? It could be a plant, or a new doorbell or the name or numbers of your house. Something that will trigger you to think the thought you want to think. Of course it could be the Laurence LB key ring.

What do you want to say about your home? Warm and fuzzy? Cool and retro? Grand and powerful? Warm and welcoming?

Examine each element of the approach to your home and see how it currently looks in comparison to the funky, retro feel you want or the warm and welcoming approach. Start from the kerb, the gate, the front lawn or garden, the path, the plants on display, the driveway, the items you have stored in front. Does the 1960s caravan that's been sitting in your driveway for the past 15 years give the impression of grandeur and power you want? Is the gnome funky and retro or a little sad? Is the broken gate the impression you want to give to friends?

What can you do about this? Does it require the expense of having the driveway completely re-laid or can you simply mow the lawn properly and re-think the borders? Would a bold splash of paint to the gate do the trick? Or would you prefer to have a whole new archway built? Can you put a fence up at the front or would some neat, boxed shrubs look more appropriate?

Think about how you would like to guide people to your front door. Do they follow a path? Is it as appealing as you'd like it to be? Is it even obvious? Don't you hate it when you don't know how to approach a building? It should be obvious so that people feel comfortable as they walk up.

How about adding light to welcome people? If the path is long, why not add light posts along the way? And the porch should be well lit. Do you prefer a traditional glass lantern or a contemporary wall light that shines closely up and down the wall enhancing the texture of the stonework? Have you considered putting lighting in the front garden? To pick out some architectural detailing in the façade of the house or simply to spotlight a tree?

Your front door is nothing short of a statement piece. Doors tell such stories. What does yours look like? The front door is a real opportunity to add a splash of colour. My grandparents had a 1950s candy pink front door and it has left an indelible impression on my mind. I'm not necessarily recommending it to you, but for me, it will always be a reminder of happy family holidays. What colour door is right for you? Do you like the gravitas of a black door, the contemporary nature of a wide, wooden door or the bright burst of happiness that a yellow door could bring?

Seaside towns in particular are fond of painting the facades of houses. In India, the town of Jodhpur (where the trousers came from) is painted entirely in blue. From the hills it is a gorgeous sight to look down on to a sea of blue. Does your road have the type of character to withstand a bright blue wall? Would you feel great about that wall or would you always be worried about what the neighbours think? The idea is to make you feel good so don't rebel if it's always going to nag at you. On the other hand, if the neighbourhood celebrates individuality then go wild.

The hardware on your door can also create quite a first impression. A knocker can be grand or entertaining. It can be traditional or extremely contemporary. You can have fun with doorbells and chimes and let people know you have a sense of humour as the James Bond music kicks in at the touch of a button. Letterboxes and house nameplates can look incredibly sleek and modern or can all but give you a hug with old fashioned welcome-ness. How do you want people to feel as they arrive at your door? Do you want them to appreciate your style, your finesse and your taste or do you want them smiling at your warmth and the inevitable plate of cakes and pot of tea that's on the other side of the door? Both impressions are there to be made.

2. Warm welcome

How does it feel as you enter your home? Is it cold and dark waiting for you to switch everything on? Is that a ritual you enjoy? Or could you set up a timed system so that the house lights are on as you enter and the entrance is warm.

What do the lights in the hallway display? This is your first impression of the home as you return to it, what is highlighted for you to see? What do you notice? Is it the state the skirting boards are in? A light bulb needs replacing? Or is it a painting that came from New York, reminding you of your Sarah Jessica Parker moment as you and some friends went shopping for a weekend in Manhattan?

Look at the lights, the colour of the walls, the skirting (this area is renowned for scuffing and can easily give the impression of neglect) and the pictures on display – these are the visual elements of this space – what do they say about you and, once you've worked that out, are they saying what you want them to?

New wallpaper in the hall will give the whole house a new burst of life. (Practical note: Bear in mind it's a much bigger space than you originally think and could lead all the way up the stairs. If you get a paper with a large pattern, you'll need many rolls.) A brave choice of paper will be a statement and will always be remembered by family and friends. Are you brave enough?

Is this area filled with down-lights only creating a corridor of lights like a runway? Or can you split up the space with some softer lighting options? A table lamp on the console, a pendant (or chandelier) in the stairwell, wall lights along the way, perhaps. And would these be wrought iron sconces or something with a putty coloured silk shade? Could the down-lights at the very least be directional so they could be pointed towards the pieces of art you have on the wall? Or the rug you've brought back from Tibet (or Tadcaster).

This is a high-traffic part of the house and will get scuffed and bruised more often than anywhere else. What is the state of the paintwork? How would a new coat look on the way up the stairs? Does the banister need another coat? Does it have to be boring old white? Have you thought about unleashing your personality on the handrail up the stairs? Maybe the carpet needs a re-think? If it's looking worn and tired, you will feel worn and tired as you tread on it. A new lease of life, maybe even a splash of colour could bring untold joy to that schlep up the stairs (and maybe even encourage the kids to bed!).

3. Efficient entrance

How organised is the area? Do you huff and puff at the sight of the cupboard every time you open the door? Do jackets lie on the floor, muddied boots carelessly strewn across it? And what is the matching glove situation like in your house? How do you feel about this one little cupboard? Does it give you an innate sense of satisfaction? Does its efficiency simply bounce out at you and hug you or is it quite a different welcome altogether?

Not only should the entrance of a home be warm and welcoming, it also has a vital role to play in terms of organisation. Storage is a key consideration and when this part of the home is under control, you feel better for it. Sometimes it's as simple as that – you feel as organised as the state of your cupboards! (I have to admit, I can be on a real high for days after a good clear out. I did my office before I sat down to write this book and the feel good vibes are still with me.)

De-cluttering is a cathartic process and as good for the mind as it is for the school run efficiency in the morning. What would you need to do to make that 15 minutes of activity a better experience? Would some hooks in the right place and a fun place to store shoes help you and the kids to get through those trying moments before you head off to school?

Case Study

Lara has three children under the age of eight and they all go to primary school. I met her at one of my Head Space (how to juggle work and home) workshops, where we discussed how to make the school run more enjoyable not only for her but also for her children. It was (in her own words) a 'daily torture'. However, she did recognise that she would be escorting her children to school every day for at least the next six years. (That's almost 1200 school-runs in the morning and another 1200 to bring them home again.) Understanding these figures alone gave her some real motivation to get it right!

To start with, we put a simple schedule in place – to give her some keys stages by which certain events had to be done (up at 7am, breakfast finished by 7.30am, dressed by 8am etc.). I recommended that she bought some clocks *with her children* so that those who could tell the time could understand these key times, explaining that it's important the children help with the shopping so they feel a certain sense of ownership of the clock (as well as to the idea).

We then designed a storage unit where all the shoes, jackets, gloves and school bags could be kept. We labelled them with a photo of the child, which they then decorated (as they do in school – something the children are used to) and created a space the kids would learn to respect.

The efficiency made Lara feel better on a logical level but she still felt an emotional void when it came to thinking about this (albeit short) part of her day. I asked her to think of something that would make her happy and she started talking about music and dancing, she also mentioned bouncing (she thinks of herself as a Tigger type character, which is a very fun but equally useful character to get into!).

Out of this discussion we created a special disco time for the family in the morning. Once the children were ready with their bags and packed lunches waiting at the door, they were allowed to put on a piece of music and dance to it. But the real winner came when they introduced a re-bounder (a small trampoline) that they could bounce on to music. Lara took this opportunity to wish them a fun day, she reminded them of all the good things that were about to take place in their day, she told them how much she loves them and how much she was looking forward to seeing them again in the afternoon.

I heard back from Lara as this 'system' started to take effect and she shared how much happier her children were as they literally bounced to school. She felt not only better about this time in the morning but positive about it. It had become one of her favourite times of day.

What times of day can you re-design with some clever storage, a few carefully purchased accessories and a disco?

Homework part 2 – take action

This initial part of your home is incredibly important. It is where impressions are made by people visiting for the first time and equally it is where you decide how you are going to feel about the house as you come in. So let's focus on this area first. I want you to do something straight away, something that will remind you that you are taking care of your home and that will make you feel good that you have begun this process.

Creating Space

We haven't started on your personal style yet or how the rest of the family fits into your grand scheme for the home but there are some givens in home design and a warm welcome and some efficient storage at the entrance of the home are as fundamental as it gets. So let's get this area sorted out before you move forward, then you'll know that you can, I repeat, you can, design your home to not only suit you but to make you feel better.

Pick one of the aspects of this area that we have been discussing and actually do something to improve it. As I don't know your house, I can't tell you what it should be. Equally I don't know your personality style so I can't tell if you're the type of person who is now going to wallpaper the entire hall area in wild chrysanthemum paper or whether you will be satisfied with changing the light bulb that's not been working in the porch light for six months now. And to be honest, it doesn't matter which you do, as long as you do something.

Taking action is an incredibly important part of this process. Reading and enjoying the book is one thing but actually making it useful as you read it is another. I encourage you now to find a great paint colour for the banister or re-direct the overhead lights to highlight the art on the walls or simply clear all the old shoes out of the cupboard to make space for some new ones. Do something and feel good for it. Make sure you celebrate that you actually did something – no matter how small. It's important that you reward yourself for your achievements and that you acknowledge that every single small thing is part of the process of creating the home you deserve.

Congratulations

You have given a great deal of thought to what home really means to you. It's not something we do often and you may well have had to put some much loved cynicism to one side for a bit, or perhaps you didn't need to and have always understood how important it is to get your environment right. Either way, going through these exercises and questions should have really helped you flesh out what you think your home should provide for you – both physically and emotionally.

You should also have actually done something, be it small or monumental. A small action to get the ball rolling will help you see that the design process is underway and should make you feel better. Check in with yourself in the morning and see if you feel better. I bet you do.

Next step is to discover a little bit more about you – what you really like, what your unique taste is and how on earth you're going to create an environment that reflects that personality. It's a fun part of the journey and really worth indulging in. I'll see you in the next chapter. (After you've changed that light bulb...)

FOUNDATION 1: PERSONAL STYLE

Space 2 – Me Space

"Be yourself, everyone else is taken"
Oscar Wilde

"I long, as does every human being, to be at home wherever I find myself."
Maya Angelou

DWELL-BEING MODEL

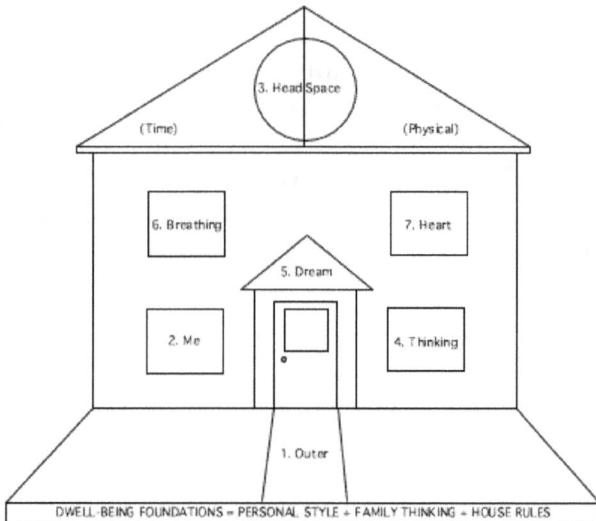

DWELL-BEING FOUNDATIONS = PERSONAL STYLE + FAMILY THINKING + HOUSE RULES

There are seven distinct spaces in a house, and an art and a science to getting each space right. The Dwell-Being system is a simple journey through these spaces, designed for you to build a genuine understanding and clear ideas about what will make your home calm, sane and outrageously gorgeous. Dwell-Being is about balance – creating structure as well as beauty, designing a house that feels good as well as looks good.

These are the steps of the journey you have ahead and what you can expect from them.

Well done, you have figured out your **Outer Space**.
o   You know what home actually means to you.
o   As you walk through your front door you can leave the world behind you.
o   Your Laurence Llewellyn Bowen key-ring inspires you and makes you smile.
o   You've changed that light bulb under the stairs.

Now it's time to discover your **Me Space**
o   You are going to create a Dwell-Being concept board – and conceive a 'signature style' for your own home.

Head Space
o   Soon you'll have an armchair or a spare bedroom to call your very own.
o   You'll also know how to find some time for yourself and some time for your home.

Then we'll move on to:

FOUNDATION 2: FAMILY THINKING

Thinking Space
o   House dynamics – how to coordinate your thinking style with the patterns and styles of the rest of the family.

Dream Space
o   Sleeping spaces – how to design places to sleep.
o   Goal design - making space to envision life as you want it.

Breathing Space
o   Chill out zones – how to craft places to relax.
o   The science of being - establishing space to connect with family and friends and to just 'be'.

Heart Space
o   Heart of the home – how to organise places to eat and be together.
o   Heartfelt communication - build space to feel, to listen, and to be heard.

FOUNDATION 3: HOUSE RULES & HOUSEKEEPING

Conclusion
o   House rules - dos and don'ts.
o   Feel confident to make changes.

Me space chapter outcome

By the end of this chapter you will have:
- Knowledge of your personal sense of style.

- A desire to express yourself (in your home and wherever else you fancy it...)
- A confidence in yourself that will mysteriously infiltrate your entire way of thinking.
- Learnt how to be at one with yourself even if you're a complete stress-head and can't even spell Buddha.

Equipment you will need for later in this chapter

- Old magazines
- Your photo albums
- The Internet

Home truth

I'm going to get to the heart of the matter. (Remember the home truth section is the 'telling it like it is' bit.) Lots of women who spend too much time in the house, can, on occasion, pick up some martyr like tendencies. We fall into the trap of making every decision for the benefit of someone else. It has become habit to consider others first, namely the children, probably followed by the dog or maybe the husband, depending on how things work in your home, then the household chores, the needs of your larger family and your friends, and finally, trailing behind in last place, you.

I doubt this is working for you. Is it working for you?

I have no doubt it is working for everyone else though and they're not going to be the ones to stand up and say, "Hey, don't you worry about me, why don't you just think about yourself for a while?" Occasionally they'll have the pressure of Hallmark bearing down on them like a ton of bricks. The cards, flowers and homemade lovelies will arrive to show you how amazing you are but for the rest of the year they'll gladly accept you sacrificing yourself in favour of them.

Because it's your job.

Except it's not your job at all. You've simply accepted it this way over the years because, when you had your first child, you didn't really anticipate the extraordinary levels of work involved in running the home and so didn't take the time to carefully allocate roles in advance. And things have just sort of crept up on you ever since.

I'm not implying here that your husband/partner or children do nothing to help at all (though for some of you this will be true); I'm asking you to think about the priorities in your life and just where you appear in them.

Priority number one

So I'll let you into a great secret – one that some of you may simply not believe (you mean chocolate is good for me?... No!). Placing yourself anywhere but at the top of the list is wrong. You have to be your number one priority. You have to think of your needs first. This isn't a case of me simply trying to make you feel good about yourself here. I'm not. I'm saying think about it like an emergency on board a flight. Please ensure that your oxygen mask is securely fitted before you assist others. Please make sure that you can breathe before you try and help others because if you don't you are of no use whatsoever.

Do you remember the training from Bay Watch? (I know... I'm sorry.) The lifeguards were always told to protect themselves with the body of the person they were rescuing. If they were heading for the rocks, for example, they'd need to turn the person into the rocks to cushion the blow for them. It seemed a bit cruel but the truth is you're not much use as a lifeguard if you're as unconscious as the person you're trying to rescue – no matter how tight your swimming costume is or how high up it rides...

Taking care of yourself is not a selfish act. I'm not asking you to jump ship here and leave your responsibilities sitting on the doorstep. What I'm saying is that your self-esteem holds a higher standing than feeding the ducks or vacuuming behind the sofa or shoe shopping for the kids or even feeding them. Your state of mind, your self-worth, how you see yourself and what you think about yourself outweighs everything else that you do. And only you can do something about that.

Me space

'Me space' is about working out who you are, who you used to be and who you want to become. It is about understanding the real you, the authentic you. Me space is giving you a few questions to think about, that will help you see yourself in the bigger picture, so you can give your home-life a fair assessment and so that you can create a home that will support your genuine everyday life and bring out your true tastes and unique style.

It might be the first time you have ever considered this, or you may do a lot of reflective work, in which case this will be easy for you but, for those who haven't done these types of exercises before, it might be a little uncomfortable. The notion I'm suggesting (indeed downright insisting upon) – that you are more important than your children - might have already offended you. Or it may come as a small relief. I suspect this relief will grow and my aim is that it will build towards creating a healthier self-esteem in you.

Home esteem

Our environment has a huge impact on our state of mind. There are some places you will have been to that may feel immediately 'like home' and others you can't wait to leave. Think about the design (or more to the point the anti-design) of the Big Brother houses. Certainly by the later series, when the psychologists had really gone to town, these rooms had been specifically created to bring about stress and tension (all in the name of good TV).

The sharp angles in the kitchen and the choice of garish colours were all cleverly thought through to exacerbate the feelings of tension and pressure, not to mention the massive, veined eye-ball that featured on one of the living room walls, (reminding them further they were under constant supervision.)

On the other hand think of a cathedral and how you enter into the small entrance, the dark wood overhead, the solemnity that hits you, the hushed tones beyond the door. And then as you walk into the main hall, a sense of wonderment takes you over, the space above you (which draws your eyes upwards, to the heavens), the light that shines through the stained glass windows, the magnificent columns, the beautiful carvings. You are in awe of it all. Surely something special exists here? Surely there is something more than me, you think. They were clever chaps those cathedral builders, were they not?

It is my belief that we should use these techniques, both modern and ancient, and put them to good use in our own homes. I'm not suggesting an atrium of awe for saint mummy here but I do think it's not out of the question that your house design is given more thought than simply putting up with the rooms – the space and the layout - that were originally conceived by a Victorian/ Edwardian/ Georgian gentleman architect and adding a coat of magnolia to the walls and a couple of brownish sofas.

If our environment can have such huge impact on us and how we feel – be it negative or positive – doesn't it make sense to harness that and put it to good use in the home? Don't you want a space that feels comfortable and welcoming or exciting and vibrant or sophisticated and glamorous or bubbly and delicious or calming and tranquil or just 'so you'? Of course you do and in order to do this you need first work out what 'just so you' actually means.

It's important to define your own sense of belonging and role in the home first then you can go on to discover a style that will bring out the best in you. It might be quite revealing, so roll up your sleeves and let's dig in.

Just so you factor

As an interior designer and someone who writes about interior design, I come across the term 'wow factor' more often than most and feel about it the way an English literature teacher feels about the word 'nice'. In its most useful capacity, I use it as an opportunity to discuss what wow factor actually means to people, (because obviously there is no historical style and formulaic design concept that results in 'wow factor'.) The wow is a response made by you and like responses to all things aesthetic it will vary from person to person.

What makes you say wow?

All of a sudden, it's obvious there is no generic answer. There is no one-size-fits-all. We are attracted to different colours, shapes, textures and patterns. We give them all different meanings, depending on our upbringing, our past, our education and our lifestyle.

Our parents' and grandparents' style may have had an impact on our thinking. Places we have seen, holidays we have been on, countries we have visited and places we have lived all have a bearing on what we like and what we don't. A childhood memory of a place that made us happy or an object that had special significance to us will have, over the years, impacted our sense of taste and become our personal style. And now, we just 'know what I like when I see it'.

However, if we're asked up front what we like, then we may find it difficult to express our particular predilections, our penchants, our partialities, our unique taste, our own wow factor.

Personal taste

I used to hate discussing my personal taste. If I was shopping for clothes, for example, and an assistant asked me which designers I liked or which brands I bought, I had a tendency to walk away hastily in a state of embarrassment and mild confusion. She undoubtedly thought I was a complete lunatic or simply rude and had no idea of the pressure she had put me under with her helpful question. On the other hand, I didn't feel she was being helpful. I couldn't hear her asking for clarity, I didn't see her need for a brief that would *help her help me* choose an item that would suit me. All I felt was judgement. What if I chose the wrong thing?

I hated that feeling even more - fearing what other people thought about me (and my choice of designer label – I mean please...) I wanted to be sure of what I liked and what I didn't but there was a part of me that needed to know the 'right' answer. Why didn't I know? What was holding me back from expressing my opinion on my own personal taste? Where was my own voice? Shakespeare with his "To thine own self be true" was busy rolling in his grave, for sure.

My husband on the other hand, has no problem whatsoever about expressing his opinion. Like it, don't like it... move on. He makes decisions with speed and determination. The idea of pondering, mulling and cogitating has no place in his world of progress and momentum. I would watch him and feel almost jealous at his ability to pick and choose. 'What if you get it wrong?' I asked him. And he gave me the most magnificent answer. An answer that set me on a great journey of self-discovery and which has led me to a radical switch in the way I think. He said, "There is no right or wrong." (Bless him.)

Actually the 'the great journey of self-discovery' didn't really start out that way. It was more of a day trip really. I'm from Yorkshire, you understand. We're not traditionally into navel gazing and working out the meaning of life, I thought (please note past tense to all deep thinking and spiritual Yorkshire folk reading this). In fact, I'd already had great opportunities to do some serious soul searching - I'd backpacked my way around the world, spent time in India, hung out with hippies (been a hippy, if only momentarily), examined ancient cultures and visited strange and spiritual cities and temples and my conclusion had still been, 'There's now't so queer as folk'.

And yet there I was, after a heart-to-heart ('why can't I do this and what makes it so easy for you?') discussion with my husband brought about by a not even remotely spiritual 'personal shopping experience' in a large department store, catapulted forward in the game of 'who am I and what on earth am I doing here?' A light bulb had gone off.

My day-trip of self–discovery turned into the inevitable (as those of you who've been on their own journey will testify) epic voyage. However 'self-discovery' doesn't have to be a never-ending game of hide-and-seek with you and your children all trying to find mummy. It's a way to live, and, most importantly, a way to think.

It doesn't require becoming all Zen and Om and dreadlocked. It's just a discovery of what makes you tick, what lights your fire, what floats your boat. Discovering what makes you 'you' makes life easier, more interesting, more satisfying and more meaningful. Discovering the value of authentic living is about doing what you're good at, what you enjoy most and what works and you can do this without being selfish or outsourcing the raising of the children and the running of your home. In short, it works for everyone. You can have your cake and eat it. Happy days.

Having your cake and eating it

I love the word authenticity. It screams personality. Uniqueness, special, well designed, destined, it has a sense of spirituality about it and yet a solidity that makes perfect sense. It means cool (so profound!). It's passionate and energetic and creative and intellectual, it's fun, liberal, insightful, and respectful and yet swears like a stand-up comic when the kids leave the room. It is naughty and risqué and partial to innuendo but equally is cultured and compassionate and competent. This is what authenticity means to me.

Authenticity is the basis from which to design a home. A home that is authentic to you. What does it mean to you?

Homework

- What does authentic mean to you? Please write your answer in a notebook (it's a good idea to date this, so you can look back later and see how much your thinking has changed and/ or progressed).
- And importantly, let my husband's answer guide you. "There is no right or wrong."

Honesty about homework

Feel free to do the homework now (ideally) or wait until the end of the chapter where I'll have all the questions hanging out together. If that intimidates you because it resembles an exam or some other such piece of paperwork of a formal nature then just answer the questions as you go along and use this time wisely rather than spending it thinking up excuses as to why you can't possibly do this. This is easy. Easy peasy lemon squeezy. Have faith.

Discovering what we're about, finding our inner Mojo (thank you Mike Myers) is frequently something we like the idea of but when we get there and it's time to knuckle down and look at the bare bones of our inner souls, we suddenly find the kitchen cupboards need a good wipe down or the nappy bin needs disinfecting. Don't you find?

Facing fears

How did you get on with the authentic exercise? Did you jump straight in, revel in the semantics, delight in your descriptions and nuzzle with your nuances? Or did the mysterious force grab you, holding you back, making you feel silly or self-indulgent or that you were 'wasting your time'? You'll excuse the more cosmic side of the author here, but the 'mysterious force' is just your ego. It's the part of you that likes things to stay exactly as you are. Right now, this minute. Despite pulling your hair out with frustration over something (your weight, your parenting skills, your choice of underwear) your ego will tell you in true better-the-devil-you-know spirit that it's not worth changing for. It likes to be in control and feels very protective of what it does. The ego does not like to be criticised and is easily bruised, which can be done as simply as bringing any current behaviour into question. It's a sensitive soul but it just needs to be handled with care.

All the ego needs is a bit of pampering and a few words of encouragement (like a young child) and it will feel all tickety-boo again. I know I sound a tad condescending here but really it doesn't require much more than this. Over thinking will lead nowhere. So just tell yourself that everything is going to be great – that the house is soon going to be outrageously gorgeous and ridiculously organised and that the family is going to benefit from huge doses of happiness and a new found fondness for one another - and then get on with the important task of making that happen.

And now on to something a little more meaningful – your taste in interior design.

Style fear

Most of us feel uncomfortable having our sense of taste and style under scrutiny. Research indicates that interior design clients, no matter how wealthy, are actually intimidated by interior designers, (people who profess to have the much sought after 'taste') for fear that their own lack of taste will be discovered. It's perfectly understandable and in fact, it's not only clients who feel this way. Designers themselves go through this fear.

For designers, it's the fear of rejection, from peers or the media or simply clients, and this happens especially when pushing the boundaries and experimenting in something new. And this is the key. It's the newness of any situation that makes it so daunting. It's exactly the same for clients; it's the fear of rejection that holds people back. What if people laugh or scoff or turn up their nose if I try something new?

It is daunting to stretch yourself and to shift out of your comfort zone. As you do so, the butterflies kick in with a mild to severe sense of nausea, depending on how you handle adrenaline. But that's what it is, your body is just responding to new stimuli. As soon as you recognise that it's a perfectly normal and extremely healthy response (your body is just alerting you to pay closer attention as it's on unfamiliar territory and a boost of concentration might be worthwhile) then you can move forward – a little uncomfortably at first but with more confident strides as you get into the swing of things.

The same applies to the first few tentative steps into designing and discovering taste. However, once you've got the hang of a few simple techniques, then you don't even think about them again and they become intuitive. But up until that point it's normal to feel embarrassingly clumsy. This clumsiness is something we need to get over and thankfully it's very easily done. It's simply a case of practice. As my saying goes, practice makes almost perfect (because perfection is a mirage and simply not worth the heartache).

How do you practise taste though? Isn't taste something we're born with? Aren't we supposed to have an innate sense of style? I really take offence at this idea. And, at the risk of shooting myself in the foot, I blame the media (I appreciate that they are an easy target and that, yes, I am a part of that milieu). As a writer I know what happens.

Media to blame?

I interview a person, I admire said person, I want them to shine, I want my readers to know what a great person they are and so I 'big them up'. I don't waste my precious column inches (or 140 characters) talking about the hardships of design practice that my interviewee went through. I don't labour the hours and hours of hard work they put into sketching and observing nature and art, I don't show off their first attempts so the world can see their work-in-progress. No. I give them an air of grace and show off their 'natural ability' and the ease with which they are now able to create.

Out of interest this is less so with athletes and dancers, where blood, sweat and tears are all part of their brilliance, but an interior designer is rarely hailed for their dedicated hours of practising their 'taste development'. No, no, no. We writers just point out their 'innate sense of style' and how naturally and absolutely fabulous they are. Case closed. My fault. Sorry about that.

So by way of amends, here is the answer to what you need to do to get the 'fabulous taste' you've always secretly yearned for. And it's not difficult.

Dwell-Being's guide to acquiring taste

Here is my 7-step guide to taste.
1. Breakdown the elements of design.
   - Shapes
   - Colours
   - Textures
   - Patterns
2. Familiarise yourself with components of design.
   - Observe them closely (you probably haven't admired a line in a while have you?)
   - Play (draw triangles – which angles please you? How about a circle?)
3. Decide which appeal. Some examples:

- Squares – yes/ no
- Pyramids – yes/ no
- Orange – yes/ no
- Shiny –yes/ no
- Herringbone – yes/ no
- Greek key – yes/ no
- Etc., etc.
4. Take favourite components. For example:
- Lines
- Rectangles
- Primary colours
5. Practise, practise, practise.
6. Develop lots of 'work-in-progress' (read rubbish you wouldn't show the cat).
7. Create masterpiece such as Mondrian's Composition II in Red, Blue, and Yellow (1930) or perhaps his more developed work 'Composition with Yellow, Blue, and Red' (1937-1942).

I know I made this sound like child's play. I truly mean no disservice to Mondrian and I know that composition, proportion, juxtaposition and form all played vital roles in his work but if you break it down to the bare facts, my seven-step process is sort of what he did. And the truth is that rudimentary skills really can bring about aesthetic magnificence.

Simplicity

Simplicity is often the most important element of design. All good designers talk about their best ideas being incredibly simple (not necessarily in technique but in concept).

'Simplicity is the ultimate sophistication."
Leonardo da Vinci (a 'good designer' by anyone's standards).

I'm not saying it's simple to find brilliance in design. I'm saying the brilliance in design is simplicity. And the simple truth is that you only know what's simple when you've done all the practice and the 'work-in-progress' and finally the simplest of ideas shines through. But I digress here. Because simplicity is not the basics. Simplicity is something you aspire to. First things first – practise.

Practise

Practise finding the elements of design that you like and once you've got this habit under your belt, you can think about what you like and why you like it with ease. Soon you'll find your own style becomes apparent, beautifully and very naturally apparent. You start to feel comfortable making choices and you learn to know what suits you and what doesn't.

Soon you'll be able to spot the exact sofa you're looking for from the shop window and the perfect picture frame you're after from a 120 thumbnail screen display. It's just a matter of practise. Practise makes almost perfect.

Homework

Unless you have small children and happen to have a lot of colour blocks and shapes, patterns and textures around for their development, it might feel a little inane to start making these 'elements of design' for yourself. (I suspect you haven't dashed off and started cutting up cereal boxes just yet.) However, I would suggest with the politest but firmest of tones that this is where you start. Taste won't just magically jump out at you. A smidgeon of learning is required. (I'll turn my teacher voice off now).

The Dwell-Being Signature Style Selector

Rather than duplicate the whole exercise here, I have produced a visual format of how to look at these elements of design in a structured format on my website. It's interactive and fun. Spend some time looking through the sections and choose which things appeal.

- Shape
- Colour
- Pattern
- Personal

You can put them on a 'virtual sample board' so that you can view them later and see how your taste is coming together. It's an opportunity for you to play and to 'warm up your eyes'.

Put some time aside – maybe half an hour - and then check it out:
http://dwell-being.co.uk/your-style/style-selector/

What did you learn?

I hope you enjoyed the Dwell-Being Style Selector. Did certain shapes, colours, patterns and textures start to appeal more than others? And did you go on to the next section that asked about your history and what impact that has had on your taste? This is a really important factor for you. While we all seek the 'designer eye' and great taste, there is no one single taste. We all have our own interpretation of it and it is our confidence in that interpretation that makes it special.

Think about it, when we first see something really new in fashion or art or interiors, most of us react quite harshly to it. It's unfamiliar. It doesn't instantly appeal. However, as we become used to it, as we start to see it around us more and more, we learn to appreciate it and soon enough we're back in ra-ra skirts or dangling Grolsch bottle tops from our boots or in love with Lithuanian crocheted toilet rolls holders as much as the media were in the first place.

But who said the idea was brilliant? Who defines the next big thing? Who tells us what's in and what's out? Someone with confidence. That's it. They don't really know any better than anyone else, they just lay claim to the idea.

The Dwell-Being guide to taste acceptance

Here's another guide – to taste acceptance. It's designed purposefully to make you feel better. Don't let the snobs tell you what's what. You have as much taste as anyone else! This is how taste is developed.

- Artist/ designer/ writer/ choreographer/ creative person thinks of new idea (after much practice!).
- Creative Person (let's call him Max) nervously shows work to peers and/ or agent seeking their approval.
- Max is laughed at horribly and retreats under his duvet.
- Or Max is lauded as genius and Max has huge confidence boost.
- Agent feels nervous at assessment and shows work to peers.
- Agent is laughed at horribly and finds gin.
- Or agent is lauded as having a great eye and has huge confidence boost.
- Max creates more work and exhibition (in relevant format – interior, performance, book etc.) is produced.
- Media assess exhibition and adds feedback – same cycle of rejection or momentum takes place here.
- Public see novel work for first time and trend followers make assessment based on what agents and media have said.
- Layman (let's call him Jeff) says "I don't get it."
- Trend followers bring Max's work into the world.
- Jeff sees it with increasing regularity.
- Jeff accepts new work as the new fashion (remember my pedal pushers 'story'.)

- Trend-setters get bored and start to reject Max's work once they see it everywhere.
- Max starts again.
- Jeff catches up sooner or later.

Opinion, opinion, opinion, conjecture, conjecture, conjecture. Nobody actually knows! People just guess with confidence. And a little confidence is all you need. Confidence in your own taste and your expression of that taste. And this is what I'm going to show you how to find.

Digging for self-knowledge

First a little digging, because confidence in yourself requires self-knowledge. How can you be sure of yourself if you don't really know yourself? How can you express your opinion, with true confidence, if you're not really sure where it came from? Self-expression requires self-exploration. Sadly, this is often portrayed as an unpleasant and gruelling experience. For the life of me I don't know why. Other than the fact that we're not very practised at it. We gloss over things, we talk about the weather, we create facades galore to protect ourselves, we smile on the outside when we're deeply unhappy on the inside but these are just habits we've fallen into. They can be unlearnt. The result of which will be confidence.

Am I oversimplifying this? You see this is where the Americans get it right. They'd be jumping up and down here and yee-ha-ing and hallelujah-ing and making a song and dance over the very notion that soon they will be confident. However, I know how you feel about yee-ha-ing and hallelujah-

ing so won't insist you go there. That being said, I do want to take this time to simply congratulate you on having come this far and if you're excited about the idea of gaining confidence then I'm thrilled. (If you are secretly thrilled too please put on some music and dance wildly around the room – put this moment of progress in your system so you feel good about what you're doing – believe me, I know it sounds crazy but that stuff is seriously what builds confidence. If on the other hand, you are a true cynic and not remotely moved to making a spectacle of yourself even if no one else is in the room then just smile to yourself – ideally visibly but even just imagining it will help).

Self-expression by its very description requires that you express something about yourself.

What would you like to say?

Yes, that's a stumbling block of a question if ever there was one, so let's try an exercise that will help you find out what's important to you.

Homework

Find some images that you love. They may be photos from your past, they could be images of accomplishments, they could be tokens that remind you of somewhere special. The important part is to find images that move you – that make you happy, or inspired, or in awe, or touched, or giddy, or proud, or at peace. Find as many as you feel necessary – you will know when you have enough – enjoy the process.

Look through your photo albums and skim through magazines and the net for images. Gather as many ideas as you can that harness who you are, who you have been and who you want to be. Have fun with this. Don't put the image of Halle Berry away just because you don't have her body. Don't put the ballerina back just because you don't dance anymore. Find the ones that instinctively appeal to you and then spread them out in front of you.

If you have done previous homework (oh now I'm testing, oh yes) then you will find that some of these images start to appeal more than others. All of a sudden certain colours will pop out. You will find patterns in the images that weren't first apparent but now seem to be visible once they're alongside another image. Spend some time editing these images down to six.

Find six wonderful, emotional pictures of what you think of yourself in the world. (And then dance around the room with music on full blast celebrating the magnificence that is you).

"When I examine myself and my methods of thought, I come to the conclusion that the gift of fantasy has meant more to me than my talent for absorbing positive knowledge."
Albert Einstein

I truly value this exercise and by a show of faith have done it myself. If you would like to see the images (along with a little of my personal history which I hope goes some way to help you understand my choices) then please visit the books section on my website: www.dwell-being.co.uk. The images there should give

you an idea of how to think about the exercise. There are no right and wrong answers and only you know what makes you jump for joy or makes you weep with regret. (Though when finding your own images I'd recommend the former, if I may be so bold.)
Spend some time doing this exercise. Enjoy yourself. Revel in the memories. Despite being called Me Space, this might be a fun thing to do with someone else, someone you want to share some stories with. Indulge a little.

Style strengths

The idea is for you to build up a collection of words and pictures that reflect who you are, what you think about the world and what you expect from your future. These are personal, unique and should have strong emotional appeal to you. These are your style strengths and make up the personal style foundation of your home.

Summary

You have worked out what authentic means to you, played with the elements of design and been drawn to certain shapes, texture and patterns over others. You have examined colour in the same way and now you have a selection of images that characterise your life. Can you see any of the shapes, patterns and colours you picked out previously or has the emotion within the image been more of an attraction than its parts? Do you feel like you are getting to know your personal style or simply yourself a bit better? And aren't you intrigued as to how this can be brought into your home and the benefits that could come with it?

Me space exercises:

○ What does 'authentic' mean to you?
○ Signature style – play with elements of design, find shapes, colours, textures and patterns that appeal to you.
○ Images of your life and your view of the world – condense to six and put them on a board where you can live with them for a while. Smile at them (yes, I'm serious, what is more neuroscience backs me up on this).

Congratulations

You have made some real progress in the world of self-awareness. It's not an easy journey sometimes, but it's so important that we do this. This is what the late Stephen Covey has to say about self-awareness (or lack of it).

"In our personal lives, if we do not develop our own self-awareness... we empower other people and circumstances outside our Circle of Influence to shape much of our lives by default. We reactively live the scripts handed to us by family, associates, other people's agendas, the pressures of circumstance - scripts from our earlier years, from our training, our conditioning."

Stephen Covey (author of Seven Habits of Highly Effective People)

Self-awareness is the beginning. Knowing who you are, what drives you, what values you have, what you like, why you like it, will give you amazing strength and conviction. Being sure of yourself will bring back some of the identity that was lost when you gave so much of yourself to others. Is it time you took a little time for yourself? Don't you think it will be better for everyone in the long run?

Me space has been about re-discovering your inner strengths, understanding how unique you are, appreciating what you have to offer, being proud of your skills and your talents and this started with understanding yourself. Now you understand yourself a little better, let's head up into the attic of the Dwell-Being system. Let's find you some time and some personal space so you can make the changes you want to make to your home and your life. I call this Head Space.

FOUNDATION 1: PERSONAL STYLE

Space 3 – Head Space

"Learn to live in the freedom of living well, being happy and not wasting time on bad habits."
Richard Bandler, co-founder of Neuro Linguistic Programming (NLP).

DWELL-BEING MODEL

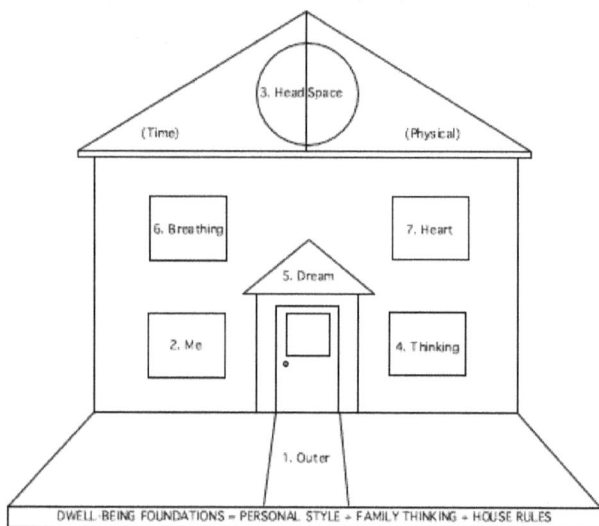

DWELL-BEING FOUNDATIONS = PERSONAL STYLE = FAMILY THINKING = HOUSE RULES

There are seven distinct spaces in a house. It is both an art and a science getting each space right. The Dwell-Being system is a simple journey through these spaces, designed for you to build a genuine understanding and clear ideas about what will make your home calm, sane and outrageously gorgeous. Dwell-Being is about balance – creating structure as well as beauty, designing a house that feels good as well as that looks good.

These are the steps of the journey you have ahead and what you can expect from them.

FOUNDATION 1: PERSONAL STYLE

You've travelled through **Outer Space.**
o You've discovered your home values and your personal meaning of home.
o You've worked on your home approach with the understanding of the power of first impressions.

Me Space
o You've enjoyed creating a Dwell-Being concept board and conceived a 'signature style' for your own home.

Now we're going to examine your **Head Space**.
o Personal space – firstly you'll understand the importance of space for yourself.
o Time design – then we'll find you some space and time to think.

FOUNDATION 2: FAMILY THINKING

Thinking Space
o   House dynamics - coordinate your thinking style with the patterns and styles of the rest of the family.

Dream Space
o   Sleeping spaces - design places to sleep.
o   Goal design - make space to envision life as you want it.

Breathing Space
o   Chill out zones - craft places to relax.
o   The science of being - establish space to connect with family and friends and to just 'be'.

Heart Space
o   Heart of the home - organise places to eat and be together.
o   Heartfelt communication - build space to feel, to listen, to be heard and to be loved.

FOUNDATION 3: HOUSE RULES & HOUSEKEEPING

Conclusion
o   House rules - dos and don'ts.
o   Housekeeping - celebrate how confident you feel now.

Head space chapter outcomes:

● Find your head space.
● Find time to think.
● Learn how to control time (I know this sounds like an impossibility but bear with me).

- Gain the awesome ability to play with your own efficiency (a truly super heroic power, second only to invisibility).
- Everything you learn in this chapter will be useful not only for designing your home but in your life, time and time again.

Home truth

We live in a world of almost miraculous communication and efficiency. At the touch of a button we know what someone thinks about a politician's speech or a celeb's short dress and her inappropriate dismount from a sport's car. We receive updates to inform us that our duvets need dry cleaning and that the local Indian is delivering for free. We travel from one side of the world to another with the greatest hassle being the shoe police at the airport. We get points for shopping, karma for recommending and friends for the listing. Life has been made simple. Carefree. Easy. Except that it's not quite true, is it? Certainly not in our line of work.

There's no vibrate mode or off switch to our reality. We're up in the night, we're on call 24/ 7, just the word 'Mummy' is enough to make us alert and 'available', even if it's not our child saying it. (Even if our child is 28.)

We count them in and out of the park and breathe a sigh of relief if all items of clothing, snacking and accessorising make it home too. We endure play dates with angels and covert ninja warriors alike and they leave without acknowledging our presence. We smile and wave and then return to picking up yoghurt pots and reloading the dishwasher. The washing machine beeps at us and we talk back to it without thinking this in any way unusual. Has Shirley Valentine returned from Greece we ask it?

Thanks come by way of repeat business. School bags are dumped at the threshold and after the banana peel has been relieved of its decorative duties from the side of the pencil case, we patiently smooth out letters requesting fancy dress costumes and pleas to man a school fair stall. We take the painting from the back of the pram and stick it proudly to the fridge. "I love your dinosaur," we shout out. "It's superman," comes the reply.

We look around. The kitchen cupboards could do with a makeover, the walls are looking really scruffy. The list we'd written of everything that needed to be done to the house. When was that? - New Year probably - sounds like a resolution type activity. The list will be under a magnet, under a dinosaur or a superman, we suppose. We decide to look for it but the phone rings. A salesman wanting to discuss the chair lift we might need for the stairs. Despite being a very youthful 39 we give it a second's thought. Would the kids love it? Would it be possible to sneak in a quick flick through a magazine on the ride down in the morning? The salesman doesn't laugh.

Does this sound like home? Of course. And is there anything wrong with it? No, of course not. It's just that there's not a lot of space left in there for you, for your plans, for your home, for your health and your ambitions. For your sanity. It's the yoghurt stained version of life and the truth is that you deserve more than the yoghurt stained version.

The 'home truth' is that the life we dream of isn't just handed to us on a plate and the home we would really like for ourselves isn't something you get from an estate agent. The good news is that you *can* create it. You *can* design a home that suits you and the life you are living or better still the life you want to live. You *can* craft an environment that enables you, empowers you and even entertains you. What is more it needn't cost you the earth. It just takes a bit of time and some structure. It also requires thought and for that you need what I call 'head space'.

Head space

Head space is thinking time. Head space is clarity. It is a de-cluttered mind that can look at the big picture and see a vision and then delve into the details and work out what needs to be done. Head space sounds like something we all long for but might be distracted from by an inappropriate tantrum or an urgent text message (or 15). I ask you:

1. Where are you going to get some serious thinking done when the majority of your household has no problem whatsoever in walking into the toilet with you?
2. Where, oh where, is the time going to come from?

Head space = personal space + time

Let's look at the easier of those two options first. Let's find you some personal space.

Personal space

Do you remember the time when you looked over at the baby, sitting in her circular playpen surrounded by toys, something to chew on, the soft book you hoped she'd be reading by 18 months? And you envied her. To have a fence around you, where you were safe, where all your precious things were next to you? Ah the joy of having some space of your own... Maybe you're still in this position or perhaps you've resigned yourself to the fact that while you look after the entire house, the cleanliness and the organisation, you don't actually feel that any part of it truly belongs to you.

Can you escape the demands that are put on you? I'm sure you've had the children invading 'special time with Daddy' episodes. And of course you've tried reading a magazine in peace (I laugh at the thought... honestly). But joking aside, do you truly have anywhere to go and think? Do you have to rely on the bathroom and a lock to get any privacy whatsoever? (Because I tried that and I had them swinging on the door handle and banging loudly on the door.) Let's take the step of carving out a physical space for you, and you alone, in your house.

If you are going to do any interior designing for yourself then you definitely need some space. While we all rely on our laptops and tablets these days, you need more than just this virtual world when it comes to interior design. You need to collect catalogues and brochures, samples of materials, pieces of wood, tiles, wallpapers and fabrics galore. Touching and appreciating texture is one of the fundamental aspects of interior design and you need somewhere to put these lovelies. It all needs space.

More importantly, however, *you* need space. You need to find somewhere, a haven if you will, that you can retreat to, where you can enter into a 'zone' your 'head space'. This head space is just for you, and you're not allowed to bring guilt and pressure into this space. In fact, saying 'not allowed' is banned. This is your space and it should make you feel like you are free – free to do exactly as you please. Just for a while.

Here are some good space options:
- A converted garage.
- A spare bedroom.
- A converted attic.
- A garden office (not to be confused with the man shed).
- A conservatory.

Here are some so-so space options:
- A dining room that is only used at the weekend.
- A well-designed corridor space.
- A well-lit desk under the stairs.
- An armchair in the corner next to a bookshelf and with access to a mobile desk – even if it's just a board that you put on your lap.

Here are some terrible space options:

- The kitchen table – you will never feel like it's yours (because it isn't – it's where the family eats) and you'll spend more time clearing it and then putting stuff back again. You'll also be horribly distracted by the chores of the kitchen.
- The downstairs loo – there really is no privacy here (as we have discussed) and we're looking for personal space not shared public property.
- Your bedroom – this is a sanctuary not a work environment. I will cover this in a later chapter, so just take my word on it for now.
- A badly designed corridor space – you'll just end up being trodden on – physically and metaphorically.

Boundaries – know your limits!

Find somewhere that is suitable for you, even if you start in an armchair and slowly take up more space as people become accustomed to what you are doing. This is important - letting people know what you are doing. It's time for you to set some boundaries.

Homework

1. Take note of how you feel about your current head space situation – give yourself a mark out of 10. Do you have anywhere you can call your own?
2. Find some space as per options above.
3. Tell the members of your family that you have found some space and ask them to respect it. (Be brave. Be bold. Take no prisoners.)

4. Spend time there. Read this book there. Do the homework I'm going to be giving you there. Make it your calm, sane head space.
5. Two weeks later, take note of how you feel about your new head space. Do you feel better? It's very likely that you do, especially if you have made your boundaries clear to those around you.
6. Do something to celebrate and christen your space.

As I've mentioned before, honestly, yes, this is homework. Recognising and celebrating these kinds of achievements is fundamental. Adopt the habit of celebrating. Put it in your neurology so that it becomes a way of life. If you can celebrate something small, you will be so much more practised at it by the time some big achievement comes along. Knowing how to celebrate is a fundamental part of happiness and to be frank, your sanity.

Case Study

In 2004, my parents moved to France to build their dream home. Mum wanted a fabulous family home in a magnificent rural setting and Dad had his heart set on designing an eco-system to create his own energy. What is more he only wanted to use local suppliers to build it and, at the time, he couldn't speak a word of Catalan. It wasn't going to be happening overnight.

It has taken them eight years to complete the place and I have to give them credit, it's exactly what they wanted to achieve. I think this is in no small part to the decision to create firstly, a personal space where they could both relax away from the mayhem and constant decision-making required. They knew there would be upheavals, (the roof coming off and an entire new floor being added) and there would be the unexpected occurrences too (the mayor turned out to be less than helpful and there were plenty of insect invasions that Mum probably wouldn't have opted for either).

Thankfully they'd had the foresight to build themselves a swimming pool first. Now while this might not be the most appropriate option for everyone, when you're in scorching temperatures and covered in dust, a pool is just where you need to go and chill out. It had always been part of their grand design but there was a stroke of genius in building it first.

Prioritise your personal space first so that when all around you are losing their head (spaces), yours is calm and sane.

Where is your personal space?

Congratulations you have found half of your head space. This, in itself, is extremely beneficial to your well-being, your sanity and your ability to move forward. Now we need to look at the other half of your head space – your time.

Time

How much time do you have?

Time passes by, tick tock, tick tock, without a care in the world. We can do nothing about it but it's a funny old thing time because while it does pass by with precise regularity, there are occasions when time stops. That moment when you know something is going to fall and break. Time can drag on forever, in the middle of the night when the baby needs feeding and time can disappear in the blink of an eye, surrounded by friends you've not seen in ages or that romantic weekend for just the two of you that'll vanish as fast as a plate of Jammy Dodgers at a three-year-old's birthday party.

Time *feels* different in all these situations. It feels like a viscous gooey journey with heavy boots on one minute and light, frothy and the shake of a lamb's tail the next. Of course it's still actually moving by at the same speed, it's just how we *feel* about it that has changed.

So if we acknowledge that time speeds up, and equally can slow down, in our perception (i.e. how we think and feel about it) then can we use this to our advantage? The short answer to this is yes.

The longer answers come through understanding:
- How we think.
- How we make decisions.
- What stories we tell ourselves.
- And the habits we create as a result.

The next few pages will take us through this and will ultimately teach you how to gain control of your time.

Controlling time

If time passes how we *perceive* it to pass then it makes sense that we need to control our perceptions. In other words, we need to control how we look, see, hear and feel. If time runs ahead when things are enjoyable and almost grinds to a halt when we are faced with the tedious and the mundane then is it possible to harness these perceptions and shape time as a result? Quite possibly! In fact the answer could be as easy as adjusting your thinking to encourage time to pass appropriately. There's just one little downside and that is when you realise that what you're supposed to be doing here is to 'think positively'. And thinking positively sounds like hard work.

Reality check on positive thinking

While I understand that there is a wide and varied selection of jobs that could fit into the tedious, mundane, even unpleasant category, aren't there times when you have no worries whatsoever about cleaning the kitchen, taking the leaky food bag out or emptying the nappy bin? Don't you just sing through these tasks *some* days?

Isn't there a state of mind that you get into that makes cooking for 12 a pleasure or clearing out the kids' old toys fun or painting the skirting boards deeply satisfying? Of course, it's not unheard of for us to focus on the horrors of our household and DIY jobs, but isn't it true that you get a certain level of satisfaction from cleaning the cupboards or de-frosting the freezer or sorting out the cutlery drawer? And what about D.I.Y? Isn't it worth it for the huge sense of fulfilment you get when you look up and see the room beautifully painted? Or when you hear someone commenting on how wonderful it looks? Or when you just feel that your home has come together a little bit more?

This is how we access the more helpful part of you, the part that will get you through the, shall we say, less-than-thigh-slapping-ly-fun times. We need to concentrate on what we are going to get out of it. We need to use our imagination or remember how we will feel when it's all done. Harness that sense of satisfaction of completing a job and put it in your pocket. Hold it somewhere safe so that you can bring it out and use it to your benefit when you next need a bit of positive thinking.

Making decisions – joys and horrors

Some decisions are given serious thought. Shall we move house? Where shall we send the kids to school? Should I look for a job? But others are less of a 'decision' and more of a 'thing you just do' - brushing your teeth for example, or turning the oven on to heat it up in advance while you prepare the food. These are less 'decisions' than good 'habits' you've got into.

There are two ways to make a decision to do something. You can imagine the benefits of it – the joy. Yes, the hallway will look much more welcoming if I re-wallpaper it. Or you can imagine the horrors of the downside – your mother-in-law is coming next week and she will be making facetious comments about the paint peeling still, if you don't sort it out.

The trick to getting stuff done is to work out what will *make* you do it -what motivates you. What does motivate you?

Motivation

What makes you get out of bed in the morning? What makes you phone the electrician? What makes you finally get the garden fence fixed? What makes you decorate the back bedroom? What makes you think you'll be really romantic tonight? What makes you think you'll do something special for the kids this weekend?

None of these thoughts are particularly 'out there'. There were no missions to Mars, no taking up Buddhism, no skinny-dipping jaunts to Brighton. Which is a shame because you're much more likely to understand your motivation for wanting to take up a new religion. You'll have given that some serious thought whereas the garden fence or the kitchen walls probably don't get quite as much attention.

The answer isn't always habit here (though probably it is concerning getting out of bed). The answer is the story you tell yourself. The story of what will happen if you do (or don't do) what you're thinking of doing (or not doing). And the story is vital.

Niki Schäfer

Story telling

Stories are incredibly powerful forms of communication. They have been used since the dawn of time to pass on information from generation to generation and so our brains are hardwired to receive data in this format and make a decision from it. We can visualise what the story entails, we hear the words and yet we also feel the impact of what is happening. We build pictures from words and feelings out of pictures. We engage all of our senses in the idea – sometimes we can even taste or smell the story.

Imagine biting into a lemon. Now picture the fruit coming up to your mouth and then taking a gigantic bite into the bright yellow, dimpled flesh. Feel your teeth digging in. Feel the juices stinging your tongue... Do you get the picture? Easily, I should imagine. But equally, has your mouth responded in any way? Did it pucker at the thought of the bitterness?   You could even be salivating (in order to get rid of the citric juices).

All this, just from using your imagination! Our minds are incredibly powerful. So let's use them to our advantage.

Homework

It's a good idea to stop and think about what gets you up and running. Is it because you like the idea of moving toward a goal (the joy it will bring) or is it because you fear what the alternative might be (the horrors)? Because we use both, all of the time, in every decision we make.

Spend five minutes and write down your thoughts. Do you move towards the joys in life or do you move away from the horrors? Do you tidy up because of the joy of seeing a clear room or because of the nagging voice you're trying to escape? Do you bake cakes with the kids because it's a fun thing to fill the time or because they'll be on at you forever if you don't? Can you see how you work towards some joys and away from some horrors? Is this the same for all decisions? Where are the differences? Just being aware of this will have an impact on your decision-making skills.

Multi-tasking

It is acknowledged that women are very good at multi-tasking. While some men have to turn the radio off to concentrate on boiling an egg, most women can juggle childcare, homework help, cooking for at least six with a few phone calls thrown in as a standard hour at the end of the afternoon. However... (oh how I hate howevers.)

The truth is that we are very good at multi-tasking while we are in one particular head space – the mummy head space for the example above. We are brilliant at coordinating projects when we have our organising hat on and we're great at creating exciting things to do when we've got the creative beret on. The problem that trips us up though, is when we try and exist in multiple head spaces. And being in two places at the same time is not a skill that has been developed yet. Unfortunately.

Focus

If we want to do something well we need to give the job our full attention. Now, while this doesn't matter quite so much for chucking a few undies into the wash, it does matter when it comes to having quality time with the kids or with getting planning permission for that extension organised. They take up two entirely different head spaces.

Are you truly aware of how you slip into different modes? How many different head spaces you access on a day-to-day basis? It's staggering. *You* are staggering.

Head space is how I define the roles that we perform on any given day. And believe me there are plenty of them. If we consider them carefully we could put them into distinct categories. Here are a few that I have observed which are likely to be part of your life but there will be others that are for your life only. Bear that in mind. You have head spaces all of your own too.

- The communication head space (telling the kids what to do, something we do to a toddler every two to three minutes, apparently).
- Nutrition head space (feeding yourself and your children – basic survival).
- Escort service (no, not that kind, I mean taxiing your children to clubs and social engagements).
- Cleaning head space (people and home).
- Organising head space (people and home).

- If you're lucky, socialising head space (talking with people you like, or at least people who are going through the same kind of things as you).
- Exercising head space (no comment).
- Volunteering head space (charity work or looking after other people's kids).
- Family-time head space (having fun with the family).
- Relaxing head space (the weekly massage you have booked, the manicure, the facial, the yoga class... oh I'm sorry, that's the other schedule I was looking at...)

(Side note: You will have noticed that I haven't even mentioned work. Because if you have a job, be it part-time, a much loved career, a start-up business or the long hard gruel of a 'necessary evil', then there are plenty of head spaces there too. I acknowledge them but I have decided to focus on the home here in this book. However, the system works just as well for working women. Use the examples in the book but adapt them to match your life.)

Defining our head spaces

Some of these words are brutal. 'Communication' and 'nutrition' define very succinctly what you are doing but they aren't a true representation of how you *feel* about the task. Let's take nutrition as an example. How do you feel about your role there? Do you think about feeding the children as 'the tedious task of getting fish fingers and something green into the little blighters' or is it a more encouraging notion 'providing the children with something healthy that will keep them going on the football pitch or the classroom'?

Can you see that the job is *exactly* the same and could be just as messy and time-consuming either way? It's just that you're thinking about it differently. Sweeping up the occasional runaway pea (OK, the whole plateful...) isn't such a bad thing when you're imagining that the children are learning the importance of a balanced diet. The chore isn't a chore anymore, it's part of a much bigger picture - the health and future of your child.

Your role as a 'nutrition provider' is motivated by your desire to have healthy kids with a healthy future. Don't you feel better for thinking about it that way?

Which leads us to the question: if you can think about tea-time in a more productive and motivating way and you actually feel good about creating kids' meals, is it possible to take a look at the even bigger picture and work out how to motivate *yourself* towards a few good habits?

Is it possible to create a healthier future for you too by changing the way you think about a few things? Don't you want to design some helpful habits, beneficial habits, habits that will work for you, as opposed to against you? Habits that after a time, you won't even think about because they'll be... habits!

Oh... but changing habits is just so difficult...it takes 21 days of concerted effort... you can't teach old dogs new tricks, right? *Wrong.* Learning new habits is all a matter of playing with time.

Playing with time

I use the words 'playing with time' very consciously. I like to play with time because while I think the idea of making more of my time (which actually is my life) is extremely important, I don't want it to feel like it's another chore. (I have plenty of them already, thank you.) I want to feel in control of time but I want to do so with a sense of humour and a sense of playfulness. Humour and play work wonders on the brain.

So how do we play with time? How can we have some fun with time and still harness it, making us feel more in control and efficient, calmer, saner?

The answer comes in two steps
- By appreciating how long things take (stopwatch required).
- By understanding the stories we are telling ourselves as we do anything (honesty required).

Let's have a look at emptying and re-loading the dishwasher (because this is something very easy to start with and because in our house it can take place more than 3 times a day, so is something I've had to 'play with' in my mind. Feel free however, to go through this exercise thinking of another chore that is more appropriate in your life.)

Step 1

The reality is it takes 10 minutes to empty and re-load the dishwasher.

Step 2

However, your mind probably thinks differently. Your mind believes it takes the whole morning. This is because your mind has concocted a terrible story to go along with the heinous chore of emptying said appliance. Your mind is stuck in the rut of 'I can't believe I'm doing this again'. 'This house is nothing but work.' 'I've got all these chores to do, so that's the day gone.' 'I can't possibly do anything for me because I've got no time.'

We create these stories of doom and gloom and before long our mind buys into them. We start to believe. We look for clues to back up our thinking and soon we become convinced that this is the 'truth'. The truth becomes the story we repeat over and over again. We have successfully convinced ourselves that the dishwasher chore is the reason we have no time. But the truth is exactly what you want to make it. It's all a matter of re-framing.

What is re-framing?

Politicians call it spin, journalists call it angle, advertisers call it positioning and life-coaches call it re-frame. It's the ability to see the same situation from a different perspective. It's the habit of always seeing the downside or it's the skill of finding the silver lining.

But how can it help us on a day-to-day basis? How does this help with the household chores not to mention the rather larger job of designing the house of your dreams?

Doesn't it make sense that if you see the *benefits* first and foremost, then you are more likely to be motivated to get on with the job? Is it truly out of the question to focus on the sense of satisfaction of having a clean kitchen (or a newly designed house) to return to once you've picked the kids up? Isn't this better than the previous train of thought, which went round and round and round your head, only ending up making you feel rubbish?

The challenge is that it also seems a little like hard work too! That's because it requires some 'positive thinking' and I have a sneaky suspicion that you aren't a huge fan of positive thinking. 'I am rich and beautiful, I am rich and beautiful, I am, I am, I am...' (Still no change?).

Positive thinking is useful (and is considerably preferable over the alternative negative thinking) but the mantras and the affirmations can be a long hard chore. Fortunately, there is an easier way to think positively. But first, let's have a look at the repercussions of negative thinking.

Negative thinking

As you know, actions repeated time and time again (a.k.a. habits) have repercussions. Habits build up and their cumulative effects have greater and greater impact.

If you leave the children's play area to sort itself out, then over the days and weeks to come it will get worse and worse resulting in a huge chore of sorting and throwing away trashed toys. However, if you tidy up a little here and there then the huge chore never really materialises. It's only a single day's debris to sweep up (which is quite enough, I should imagine).

If you leave the post lying on the front door mat then it will pile up day after day until it is an overwhelming mass of bills and missed special offers. If however, you take a couple of minutes to look through the junk mail you may well find a discount that is indeed too good to be true.

If you ignore the broken gate and the peeling paint on the front door, you will walk into your home reciting a negative mantra 'This place is a dump', 'Why is there so much to do here?' 'I can't be bothered, if no one else is going to do it, then I won't either.' Soon enough, your repetitive thinking will turn into a habitual thought. Before you know it, you're barely aware that you are badmouthing your home in your head. And once you are no longer aware of your thoughts, do you really think you are controlling your actions?

Actions follow on from thoughts. You simply do what you've been thinking about. (Isn't this true?) And when it comes to the scenario above and your negative feelings about the home, it means that you neglect it. You just let it decay. Your actions are actually inactions. And your inaction is a result of your dislike for your home. And if you think that is bad enough, what impact do you think this is having on your kids? What have you taught them without realising it? And honestly, why should they respect your home if you don't think it's worth the while to bother yourself?

It's worth thinking about, isn't it?

(***Time out*** *- You may well be considering what all of this has to do with interior design - and you'd be right to ask - but while your roles and your time have little to do with colour palettes and lamp shade choices, they have an enormous amount to do with the sanity levels in your home. So bear with me!*)

Blessed relief

You will be pleased to hear that while the vicious cycle of negative thinking that I've just described sounds exactly that − vicious, the virtuous circle of positive thinking works just as well, and is also exactly that − virtuous.

A quick tidy up at the end of each day saves the humungous effort involved at the weekend. A story read quickly at bedtime every night leads to a child interested in reading. A twice-daily brush of the teeth leads to healthy gums. A sales call a day leads to business leads. An apple instead of a chocolate bar a day leads to a deficit in calories. A kiss as he walks through the door means a habit of feeling welcomed. Five minutes of really listening to what the kids did today leads to them believing you are interested in them. Loose change in the money jar leads to a nice handbag at the end of the year.

Believe me, my cynical and sarcastic banter-filled world knows that some of these sound like bumper car stickers. And I don't advocate bumper car stickers. What I do advocate though, is being responsible for your habits.

It is so easy for habits to escape us. Because they only take a few days to create and then they get hidden – somewhere in our subconscious – and we forget about them (do you really think about the arduous habit of putting your knickers on, for example?) If we're not careful with them, if we don't take them out and give them a bit of a dust off from time to time then they can lead us down the wrong path.

It's worth giving your habits some thought. Fortunately there's a method to this, what is more, it's free of charge.

Head space and the stories we tell ourselves

What are the different roles of your home life? (If you are employed you can define your work roles too but I'll focus on just the home roles for now). Wife/ partner? Mother? Taxi driver? Cook? Cleaner? Home organiser?

Now tell me how do you feel about those words? Personally I am not at all fond of the word mother. You might think completely differently. That's the whole point of this exercise. What does mother mean to you? Do you prefer mummy or mum, ma, mater or your first name in fact? (I think it's hilarious when my kids call me Niki but only as a one off.) But let's take it a step further back because it's less about what your children actually call you and more about what you call the role itself. In your head. What are the words you use to describe this role? Not to other people but to yourself, when you are thinking about the things you do as a mother? What story do you create in your own mind?

The media has given us all kinds of mother options to choose from – do you see yourself as one of them? Are you a carbon copy of your own mother? (Or is that a really scary thought?) Are you aware of your grandmother's thinking in the way you are running your home? Is this really frightening you now or are you actually proud of that fact? Maybe you have created the role for yourself from books you have read, some fiction and romantic, others practical and useful? Who is the mother character in your mind? Give this some thought.

Now here's the hard work – because it requires honesty. Is the character you have created for your role as mother helping you? Or is she, just perhaps, being a bit of a hindrance? Is the idea that you have, about children needing you *every minute of the day,* doing you any favours? Is the thought that you are in 'control' of the children's lives serving you? Is the notion that you look after everyone but yourself, 24/ 7, helping you? Or is it actually a painful thought? Is it really just fuelling the flames?

OK, let's look at the home. How do you see your role in the home? Are you the housekeeper? Do you get phone calls from salespeople asking to speak to the owner and think 'they'll need to speak to my husband because I'm more of the home help...'? Do you view your time in the home as one long slog? Is home just a list of chores waiting to happen? Do you slip into that dour old maid role that the media has given us of housekeepers? Or are you Bewitched or Mary Poppins, capable of organising the playroom with the twinkle of a nose or a cheery tune? Which do you think would be more useful? Truthfully?

How do you think about interior design and decoration? Is it the nightmare of DIY or the magic of watching a space being transformed into something that suits you and will help you live a better life in your home? Would imagining having Laurence Llewellyn Bowen at your side help you at all? Perhaps George Clarke (a personal favourite of mine)?

How do you think you would have to think in order to think better about what you are doing? I am going to show you how to capture those thoughts and use them to your advantage when you need them the most.

Capturing thinking

Let's start with something fun. How do you think about the really fabulous things you do? You're heading off for a spa-day with the girls, for example. How do you think about that? (Get over the incredulity first – yes, this is happening, you are going to the spa.) Now how do you think about it? How do you see yourself? Do you imagine the relaxation? Do you picture the pool and the loungers? Have you got a massage in mind? Perhaps a manicure and what of the chats you will be having with your friend as you sit in the Jacuzzi and laugh about how the other half live? Where is your 'head space' now?

Isn't it easy to slip from one space to another? Relish the fact that you are capable of doing this because this is a big part of the solution. You can turn on Jacuzzi mode whenever you feel like it. You don't have to play dour maid when there's another far more attractive role you can play, even if it is just in your head. Remember, your imagination is incredibly powerful and if it can react to the lemon, it can react just as well to the bubbles at the spa.

Stories in your head

Head space is just another term for the story you are telling yourself. If you are telling yourself it's going to be easy, relaxing and hugely beneficial to everyone involved, the likelihood is you will be motivated to get on and do it. If, on the other hand, you view the job in the same way you view nail removal, you're not going to be leaping at the opportunity with the same level of enthusiasm. The choice is yours.

Head space home truths

What are the roles that make up the 'you at home' person that you are. I've mentioned a number already and I'll show you the method using these first, then you can do your own version in a way that makes sense to you.

Some 'home person' roles (now doesn't that sound attractive?)
1. Communication
2. Nutrition
3. Taxi driver

4. Housekeeper
5. Exercise
6. Social life

As we have said, these do not sound terribly attractive and if we leave them here in this state for much longer then I suspect nothing will ever get done again. So let's work on what each of these really mean and how you can look more favourably upon them.

How to re-frame the roles in our lives

1. Communication

How often do you tell your kids what to do? (I know, really, it's laughable). It's a constant stream of direction and in my world (please don't judge) occasional yelling. Time and time again they need to be told to pick up their shoes, to brush their teeth and to get their bags ready for school. And because you are a good and loving parent, you will always have to do this, until the magic day arrives and you notice that they've actually got it (or they've left to go to Uni). It's a chore.

But given the fact that you have opted for this parent role (come hell or high water) and communicating with your children is a fundamental part of that role, it seems only sensible to focus on the high water aspect of it rather than the hellish bit. Don't you agree?

Why is it that you repeatedly tell your kids what to do anyway? Is it because you want them to be self-sufficient, capable and prepared human beings? Or is it simply because you don't want to have to do the teeth brushing *for them* for the rest of their lives? Either way, it's in your best interest to encourage them to do this as quickly as humanly possible. And for that, communication is necessary. But do *you* have to see it that way?

Painful lessons

My old communication role was 'sergeant major' - especially if I was stressed. 'I have to tell them what to do all the time' was how I used to say it in my head. And it didn't work.

Firstly came the horror of hearing myself in them. When your children are yelling at their dolls to get their shoes on, you know that's only come from you (from the mouths of babes and all that). This brought about clarity - what I say and do is what *they* think is 'how it's done'. Oh help. 'Stressed me' was how they had started to communicate with their dolls. And I did not want this to be the case.

So I learnt to see my communication role in a different way. Instead of being a sergeant major, I played with the idea of being a coach or a cox in a rowing boat. Now a coach can certainly shout from time to time, but her heart is in the right place. There's focus and a vision for the team and for me personally (and I stress this is for me only, because you might see the word 'coach' and picture a bus with 51 seats) I started to think about the family more in terms of a team. And Schäfer United was born.

Yes, I have just labelled my family as a football team. But no, we don't have colours, we don't have a motto and we don't have a shield. I've not taken it to that level but there's no reason why I wouldn't because they would all help with the notion that we work together. And that is something that I will encourage them to believe.

Can you see how I have shifted the role? Can you see how my role as the family communicator has gone from scary sergeant major with loud booming voice to a much more focused sense of direction and more positive way to communicate? The coach of Schäfer United is a much better frame of mind. For me.

Pussycat

What's your style of communication? And is it working for you? Do you actually secretly want to be more of a sergeant major, to take some control over unruly kids? Have you been a pussycat of a leader and now your children have you wrapped round their fingers? Is it time to start thinking a little more in 'military terms'? Do you want to instil some discipline and show them who's boss? Routine and discipline are fundamental to a happy and healthy household and a shift in your mindset could really take away some of the pleading on your behalf and intolerance on theirs.

We are, of course, all different in how we operate our homes and I'm not suggesting there is one solution (certainly not sergeant major). I'm saying that if you feel the way you have been doing it up until now isn't working anymore, a change in thinking could help you.

I will look at the 'housekeeper' role next (because this is most relevant to Dwell-Being) but I won't go through all of the others. However I encourage you to do so. Play with how you see the roles you have given yourself. Examine which bits are working for you and which aren't working so well. Create characters and change the phrases you use time and time again in your head. Be aware of them and then shift them into something more helpful. Be playful with this. Enjoy it. Pretend you're the casting director of a play and work out your 'cast'. Only employ the best actors and actresses to perform your roles. Have fun with this. It will really contribute to creating a character you enjoy playing.

2. Housekeeper

I hear the term 'housekeeper' and I see a grand old house, Downton Abbey if I'm feeling very grand, or a drab, grey mansion from Victorian times if I'm feeling less generous. The housekeeper who works there, is lonely, if not own right miserable and her fingers are worked to the bone. What's going on inside *my* head doesn't leave me feeling all warm and fuzzy about the prospect of being a housekeeper, that's for sure.

Housewife is a term I also dislike with a passion (what, am I married to the damn house?) and the research I've conducted around the word brought about some extremely negative feedback. How do you feel about being called a housewife? Home executive was offered on a plate by some ridiculous optimist and was laughed at by most. SAHM (stay at home mum) seems to be the acronym du jour and I guess it describes a lot of the women of today in as basic a way as housekeeper once did (as long as you understand what it stands for, of course.)

SAHM

The stay-at-home mum has a funny ring about it. Of course it implies there has been a choice to stay home and raise the family but there's also that sniff of cabin fever about it. Stephen King might have coined the term perhaps. How do you see the role? Are you a little more positive about it or do you dislike the notion of being 'stuck indoors'?

I re-framed the housekeeper role of life into something vaguely palatable by slotting the term interior designer into the definition. This automatically gave the job a different slant – a hint of glamour even. I've always been a fan of homes and have lived in many but looking after them on a day-to-day basis wasn't what I was interested in. It wasn't until I was studying ergonomics that I appreciated how beneficial design can be to removing the utterly tedious and mundane aspects of my housekeeping role.

Understanding flow and how to organise the efficiency of a room, and hence the people in it, is a vital part of interior design. (This was the germ of an idea - the idea that has grown into my business concept and the ideas in this book.) I suddenly saw that I was designing my life within four walls as opposed to the house dictating to me the agenda for the day.

That being said, you can't design away all the chores, the beds still need changing and the dishes need to be washed. (Unless you delegate these jobs of course, which is a super suggestion if you can afford it. Always, I repeat, always delegate what you don't want to do, especially if you're not good at it either).

However, there is reality, and we can't all afford to have cleaners and people who kindly remove us from the daily jobs that come upon us no matter what. So, it's a matter of re-framing, of thinking about it differently.

Homework

Your homework is to look at the roles you have created for yourself in the home and see if you can shed any rosier light on them. Turn them round and have a good play, examine them from a historical perspective, or a cartoon style, it's up to you to see how changing your *thinking* about them will change how you *feel* about them. Once you feel differently (assuming it's a step in the positive direction) then your motivation towards achieving them will also change. It will happen almost magically.

Take each of these roles plus two you have created yourself, and re-frame them into a character or role that you like the look or sound of.

1. Communication
2. Nutrition
3. Taxi Driver

4. House administrator
5. Mum

Home truth – where's the time?

Having defined your roles and turned them into something that is truly of benefit to you and your family, you will have a much better understanding of why you are doing what you are doing. This sense of purpose is what motivates us. So now you've found your motivation, how do you find the time? Wasn't this the point of the whole exercise in fact? (Too true.)

You might not even need to 'spin' how you feel about redecorating your home. You may well consider this a pleasure or a hobby that you'd love to spend more time enjoying, it's just that you've got so many other demands on you.

While it's true we all have demands on us, it's also true that some people still manage to achieve about three to four times more than others who have, on the surface, the same 'demands'. Why is this?

It's a simple matter of understanding how to make the most of your time. In the corporate world, this is called time management.

Time management methods

There are several simple methods of managing your time. An effective method to save time is to bundle your jobs into a block or chunk of time. This means you do all similar jobs at the same time – cleaning jobs together, emailing done all at the same time, phone calls in one stint, cooking in bulk, an almighty ironing session. While we are always so proud of our ability to multi-task, it is in fact far more efficient if you do one thing at a time, get it done quickly then move on to the next. Clearly it was a man who came up with this idea, and when you're breastfeeding the baby, while discussing your sister's wedding with your mother on the phone and cooking your toddler's lunch, you know what you can tell that man. However, he might just have a point when you want to plan ahead and think about how to find time in your hectic schedule.

School timetable

Try thinking of your day like you used to when you were at school – in 'periods' – slots or chunks of time. Monday 9-10 chemistry. 10-11 Maths 11-11.15 break. 11.15 – 12.15 Geography. That type of thing. Would it occur to you to ask your chemistry teacher about geography? I doubt it. And would you spend your precious break time thinking about Maths? Well only if you have a certain kind of mind I guess. The likelihood is that you kept each subject matter quite distinct and then moved on to something equally enthralling after lunch.

Now you know how to make each of your subjects/ head spaces/ roles (housekeeping, nutrition etc.) if not enthralling then at least motivating enough to get them done, you can start grouping them into a schedule of efficiency and one of single-mindedness.

It's all very well to do a few household chores while the kids are around but if, time after time, you are taking up what they consider to be your 'relaxing and having a laugh with the family time' into 'let's tidy up your bedroom', then they won't be very pleased. More to the point you'll lose out on the genuine pleasure you can gain from thrashing the kids at Buckaroo or Guess Who? Isn't that why you had kids in the first place? Surely it wasn't all legacy and tax reasons, there was a sense of reliving your youth in there too. So make the time to do that.

Equally don't waste your quiet time on cleaning up the house if you have a creative project to get going with. Leap at the opportunity of an empty house to do what you truly want to do. Surely you can squeeze in the dishes later when you're cooking tea? Use your multi-functioning mind to its great potential. Make it work hard. Why do one mundane thing when you can do three at the same time? However, don't ruin a 'special' time (solo time, husband time, family time, friends time) with chores. There's plenty of time to do them later and if you don't think there is then you need a school timetable. We'll get to that soon.

Firstly, it's important to have a good understanding of what you need to get done. If you're a list writer, you're a realist and the likelihood is that you are already on top of this bit of your life. You may not have worked out previously *why* you have been doing what you were doing but you probably enjoy being the organised one and maybe even get a little thrill from crossing something off that list. No shame in that. In fact, the more little details you learn like that about yourself, the easier life becomes, because soon you know what you need to do to feel good. But we really are rushing ahead of ourselves here. Let's get back to 'to-do' lists.

Homework

You need the time to do this properly. You cannot stop half way through this process. (You have been warned!) This may at first seem a little overwhelming but the idea is not to overwhelm but to take control of the reality, so have faith and do the homework one step at a time.

We are going to create a school type timetable for your home. Presumably you went to school so you are therefore familiar with the concept. Here's what to do.

The Dwell-Being timetable

Step 1 – De-clutter your mind

Write down everything you would like to do in a day (you can do week if you're super keen but let's just start with a day). Get up, do 200 press-ups, feed the goldfish, have coffee, vacuum the living room, get the kids ready for school, do their homework for/with them, read a magazine, go food shopping etc. This is your life so you know it best. Be thorough though and write a full list of everything you do and/or want to achieve. It doesn't have to be in order, it can be random thoughts. It is important that you do this on paper. It's also best not to walk off at this stage because you'll have filled your head with the 'million and one things that need to get done' and your brain might not appreciate that.

(Again, this method works perfectly well for work as well as the home, so please write your work to-do list in the same way.)

So 'de-clutter' until you can literally think of nothing else. Done?

First things first, it's important that you look at the list and see that it's not actually 'a million and one things' after all. But still give yourself credit – there is plenty there. It's a delicate balance between appreciating how much you do (congratulations) and also not letting your brain go over and over it, which to all extents and purposes, is what makes it feel like you're tripling, quadrupling, quintupling the load. So see the list for what it truly is. It's ample but manageable. Now here's how to manage it.

Step 2 – Head space definition

Define your different roles in the way we have just been discussing – use language that *will* get you out of bed in the morning (as opposed to the soul-destroying ways you may have previously categorised your existence). These are jobs that need to be done and if you choose to be the one to do them, then casting the best light on them is the most helpful way to think about them.

Here are some examples of roles we've discussed. Please adapt them to how you want to see the role, change them to suit your life. This is important. It's about how you feel about these roles. Not me. I might think being the family coach is the most powerful way of thinking about it. You might see a bus. You might hear the word communication in a very different way. Maybe you think of an efficient telephone network or work in a world of algorithms. There is no one answer. How do you want to see and to feel about these roles?

Here are some suggestions:

1. Communication = Family coach
2. Nutrition = Children's energy provider
3. Taxi driver = Chat show host
4. Housekeeper = Interior designer and efficiency guru

Step 3 – Put like with like

Go through your to-do list and put each job into one of your head spaces (your beautifully defined roles). If you need extra categories that's fine but the idea is to condense the load. You want to be putting all your children-organising jobs under the umbrella of say 'Family coach' and all your household chores under the category 'Back off, it's Blitz time'. All your jobs should neatly fit into the categories you have made up for yourself.

Step 4 – Add colour

For those who aren't hugely visual, this next step might feel unnecessary, but I suspect that if you are reading a book about the home then you do have a view on how things look, so having visual impact will be good for you. Adding colour to the timetable will allow you to see blocks of time easily. So go ahead and allocate a colour to each role – scarlet, mauve, buttercup and peacock or just the plain primaries and secondary colours. Again this is up to you. (However, it's worth noting that if you put your calendar on a computer, you will be limited to the colour choices available. Equally, there are only so many colours on those pens you click and change.)

This is important for the schedule because it means you can see at a glance what each block of the day entails. And you can see your motivation behind it, because you've already given that an enormous amount of thought. So allocate a colour that represents how you feel about the role. Yellow for taxi driver? Does that make sense to you? Blue for home pride or maybe purple? Nutrition could be green (or pink if you see yourself in the fairy cake world). The colours can add to how you perceive the task. I use blue for communication because it feels efficient. Try blocking out your early mornings in blue and feel in control of the school run. Now that's an accomplishment! Feel happy in your choices.

Step 5 – Be single-minded

Creating blocks of time is a fundamental part of all time management programmes. Trying to do everything at once is an inefficient way of getting things done. The problem is that we women seem to take great pride in our juggling. But juggling can be very stressful, so just juggle when it's absolutely necessary (or fun) rather than on an hourly basis.

The way to deal with this is to see jobs in blocks. If you are in the frame of mind of getting the house spotless then do all the cleaning jobs in one block. Don't put the dishwasher on and the washing machine on then go and try and relax in between the two bleeping away at you. Use the timers to get all the house jobs done. If you have to get lots of phone calls made to sort out something to do with schools for the kids, don't do it when you're trying to cook for the family. Enjoy your role as the chef. If you have spare time when something is steaming or rising or braising then sort out a quick cupboard. You're in chef mode so do chef stuff.

When you're being taxi driver don't bemoan all the jobs you've got to do at home. Once you've got the hang of this system you will know that you have already planned ahead and there is time in the schedule for you to email a friend or write the kids thank you letters for them. Instead, enjoy the short time you have in the car with the kids. Think about what they would like to do in that time. Talk about their friends at school? Play a game? Listen to music? Sing at the top of their voices? Getting out of the car and thinking 'that was fun' is something that will travel with you for a while. Getting out of the car and feeling stressed because you aren't doing what you need to do is of no use to you whatsoever. You have to do the car journey, so you may as well use it productively, especially if it's also fun.

Step 6 – Organise blocks

Try blocking out a normal day using the colours you have chosen for each type of role. How does it look? Is it one slither of colour after another or three substantial blocks? To be efficient try and create a few large blocks. Do all your similar jobs at once. We get ourselves into head spaces where we think in a different way so once you've got into one head space, do all the jobs you can to do with it, before moving to another. Obviously you can return to the head space again later in the day - Lara Croft cleaner extraordinaire after breakfast and Lara Croft cleaner extraordinaire after dinner but try not to merge her with the Lotsa Huggin' Bear mummy time you have when you're breastfeeding your baby.

The head spaces are distinctly different and need to be organised so they work well with each other. Can you see that?

Step 7 – Looking ahead

Once you start to see your days as blocks of time, or even blocks of being in a certain head space, it will start to become more apparent when to arrange which activities. You can look down at your week and see that all your mornings are about efficiency, followed by a spree of house pride, wrapped up in a Hairy Bikers cook-a-thon in the kitchen. You have an hour to spare before school pick up and then it's back to being Tom Hanks in Big until dinnertime.

Did you spot it? There was a definite hour free in there sometime. Where on earth did that come from?

Revelation

All of a sudden, you will start to find free time. Where previously you've been wrapped up in one long thought about how much you've got to do, you now have a sense of control over the activities of your day. As you practise this you will become more aware of how much time each of these activities take (you can time them if you're that type of person). You get a grasp of what takes time, where you're likely to be interrupted, where other tasks might suddenly make themselves evident. You get an understanding of what you need and as you do, you learn to forward plan this into the next week's activities. 'No point in trying to do the conversation with the plumber if I want to genuinely listen to what Aileen's got to say over coffee' you might suddenly say to yourself. And you realise that you are becoming efficient.

This is a system that creeps up on you slowly but the more you use it, the more momentum it carries and before you know it, you are planning the weeks and months ahead, even Christmas, with military efficiency. Except that it doesn't feel like a military operation, it feels like home. It feels good to be on top of things.

So back to that spare hour... What are you going to do with it?

Spare time – who'd have thought?

This is when extra jobs that you've been putting off forever can suddenly find a home. Or this is where those nice extras you've been dreaming about doing but have felt guilty for taking up precious tidying-up time can go. There is time after all.

Designing and decorating a home can be one of these things. (Of course I would say that, wouldn't I?)

Look ahead at your schedule and create a block of time for interior design (or Laurence Llewellyn Bowen time if you prefer). What does that head space require? How do you want to feel? When is the best time of day to do it? When there are kids around or when you're by yourself? When the house is a mess – what do you care, you can't see it - or when the place is immaculate and you have no pangs of ironing guilt? If you create the head space first you can learn to fit these things very neatly into your diary.

You'll know how to map ahead and put projects into place. You'll feel confident that you can take on new roles and that you will be truly capable of seeing them through. You'll look at the house and think, 'I can find time to make this the home I want my kids to grow up in'. You'll look at the kitchen and think, 'I can find time to make this space work better for me, more efficient and organised so my life is easier' and you'll look at your own space, your 'Me Space' and think, 'I've got somewhere of my own. I've got space to think.'

Because when it comes to interior design, there's plenty to think about, not only in terms of finding a style to suit you but something that will please the rest of the family, something that will actually bring out the best in your family. But before we move on, make sure you do the homework. It's a crucial part of the process and is purely for your benefit. (And if that doesn't make me sound like a Sixth Form teacher getting you to fill out university forms then I don't know what would. It's your future though...)

Homework summary

Head space = personal space + time

Find your own space

- Take note of how you feel about your current head space situation.
- Find some space.
- Tell the members of your family that you have created some of your own space and ask them to respect it.
- Take note of how you feel about your new head space situation. Recognise that you feel better and truly enjoy it.

Find your own time

- Write the to-do list that's been bouncing around your head forever. De-clutter your mind. Get the list on paper.
- Define your roles (in a way that will work for you, not anyone else!)
- Put all the items on the to-do list under one of your role titles.
- Add colour.

- Group activities into longer sessions in the same head space.
- Plan ahead and carve out time in the future for the things you love to do.
- Feel good about this and practise it always. The more you use it, the more effective you will be. And soon it won't even feel like 'effective', it will just feel normal and you'll be amazed at how much you're doing and how much fun you're having. Now how did that happen...?

Congratulations

You should now have a space you can call your own. You should have a clear idea about what motivates you, some thoughts on how you think and an insight into the stories you tell yourself – good and bad. And all of these should contribute to you being more in control of your time because you have learnt how to alter your perceptions of time.

You should also have established a timetable system for your own time. It could even be in glorious technicolour. Be proud of what you have organised. It may be your first attempt but it's the starting that really counts. Make changes every week, fine-tune your system, and learn what works best for you. This system is designed for you by you. It's based on your own understanding of yourself and how you think. If it's not working then only you can figure out the way to motivate yourself. Isn't that a thought?

FOUNDATION 2: FAMILY THINKING

Space 4 – Thinking Space

"Home is not where you live, but where they understand you."
Christian Morganstern

DWELL-BEING MODEL

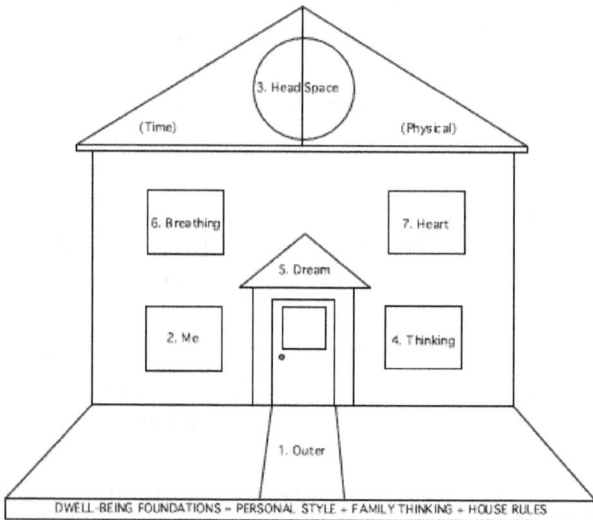

DWELL-BEING FOUNDATIONS – PERSONAL STYLE + FAMILY THINKING + HOUSE RULES

These are the steps of the journey you have already completed and those you still have ahead of you and what you can expect from them.

FOUNDATION 1 – PERSONAL STYLE

Congratulations, you have built your first foundation – personal style.

Outer Space
o   You know what home really means to you.
o   You can close your front door and feel like you've left the world behind.

Me Space
o   You've discovered you do have a taste and style of your own and have collected a number of images to represent your signature style.
o   You know that this extends far beyond the design and decoration of your home – into how you think.

Head Space
o   You have created some space for yourself.
o   You have the tools to find the time to do something just for you.

FOUNDATION 2 – FAMILY THINKING

Building the next foundation requires designing the following spaces into your home:

Thinking Space
o How to combine your thinking style with how the rest of the family think and behave.
o Appreciating what others need from the house.

Dream Space
o How to design places to sleep.
o Making space to envision life as you want it - your dreams, goals and aspirations.

Breathing Space
o How to create places to relax.
o Establishing space to connect with family and friends and to just 'be'.

Heart Space
o How to organise places to eat and be together.
o Building space to feel, to listen, to be heard and to be loved.

FOUNDATION 3: HOUSE RULES & HOUSEKEEPING

Conclusion
o A bit of housekeeping.
o House rules - dos and don'ts.

Thinking space chapter outcome

In this chapter you will learn:
• How to balance your unique style with the taste of the other members of your household (whether you think they have any taste or not!)

- How to understand the way other people think so you can appreciate their methods and reasoning and learn to live with them more easily.
- How to start believing that a house can work for everybody in it.
- How to use voodoo-like tactics of persuasion to regain a sense of control over your home.

The fable

The man looked around his small home. His wife was cooking at the stove in the tiny kitchen. His smallest child slept in the cramped bedroom next door where they all slept together. His two sons played noisily in the corner. The man tried to rest after a long day at work. How he longed for a bigger home.

The next day he went to visit the wise old woman who lived in the village. He told her of his wish for a larger home, somewhere he could be proud of, somewhere he could get some peace.

"What should I do?" he asked the old woman.
"There are three steps to climb before you find peace in your home," she replied.
"What must I do?" he asked again eagerly.
"Ask your mother-in-law to move in to your home," she answered him.
"My mother-in-law?" he said, "Have you met my mother-in-law? She'll eat us out of house and home and she snores. I can't invite her into my home, there's no space..."

"Then you will not find peace in your home and you have failed," said the wise one. "Accept her into your home and then return when you feel the need again."

"OK, OK," said the man and he returned to his home and told his wife the news.

A few weeks went by and the man could bear it no longer, his nights were now tormented by the suffocating sounds of his wife's mother's sleeping habits and her dietary needs were crippling his weekly budget.

"I need a bigger home," the man pleaded with the wise woman. "Tell me what I must do."

"Invite your chickens and your goats into the home and live with them as you do your children," came her reply.

Knowing better than to question her, the man thanked her for her wisdom and returned to his home and let the poultry and the goats in through the front door.

Only a week went by before he again felt the need to return to the old lady.

"I am losing my mind," he said. "My house is a farm yard, the floor filthy and my bed has been taken over by the chickens. Tell me, what do I do now? What do I do so I can get peace in my home?"

"Invite your brothers and sisters and cousins to stay, fill your house with family and strangers alike. Let them eat from your table and drink from your cups."

"And then..." he asked hesitantly, but the old woman ignored him and he returned home to tell his wife of the developments.

As the house rocked with laughter and the neighbours spilled on to the street, the wife was still cooking and the mother-in-law was asleep with the chickens, the man slipped away to visit the wise woman one more time.

"Please," he said. "My house has been taken over. This is driving me crazy. Please, please, tell me what I must do."
"Send them home," said the wise woman. "Ask your mother-in-law to return home, put the chickens and the goats back into their yard, and ask your brothers and sisters, cousins and all the strangers to go back to their homes."
"Then what?" he asked the unresponsive woman.

The man returned to his home and asked his family to leave and returned the animals to their pens and escorted the last drunken stranger from the premises and he collapsed on his chair and looked around him. His wife was quietly cleaning the kitchen, his youngest child slept in the room next door and his two other children sat at his feet.

"Peace at last," said the man.

Home truth

We are getting married later and later. Which means we've had homes (or rooms) of our own where our routines have become well established and our tastes have emerged, one way or another. We have formed habits. We have cultured them lovingly. We do things the way we like to do things and no one thinks twice about it.

One day, in a flush of romance, we move in together. Random bachelor items are scoffed at and quietly put to one side (ideally the attic) and girly paraphernalia is reduced by 50 percent so that he too can have some toiletries space and somewhere to hang his suit. It doesn't take long to learn that we don't approach brushing our teeth or catering to each other's family in exactly the same way and discussions ensue. We either iron out these basic details or take an early exit realising what lies ahead.

While both parties are still working, the house (or flat) is designed around evening and weekend needs. The fridge contains a small jar of curry paste, a bottle of wine and if you're lucky in the morning, milk that is within its sell-by date. The kitchen sees more take-aways than three-course meals but it works for the occasional get together of friends and, as long as there's a dishwasher, no one is complaining. The bathroom is a hotchpotch of mixed towels but once an investment in storage of some nature takes place then toiletries soon learn to live together. The guest room is used as a general dumping-ground-cum-office until a friend stays the night when boxes are pushed to one side so the sofa bed can be pulled out. This is only done before 1am if it's a parent staying and there might even be a clean towel left on the end of said bed.

The living room is a Mecca to the collection of CDs and DVDs that are someone's pride and joy, made obvious by the way they have been alphabetised or colour coded. They're all on a gadget that can fit into a shirt pocket now of course but there is still great pride in the display of such taste and acquisition and it's a natural talking point at parties.

Assuming that a relative level of harmony has reigned over these first few happy years or months in the home together then marriage takes place. A honeymoon and further holidays are had, pictures are taken, memorabilia is collected, and shortly the good news is announced.

Sometime during the third trimester a sense of panic kicks in. The desire to create a nursery more beautiful than the world has ever seen before becomes uncontrollable. The nesting instinct overwhelms the previously not-terribly-fussy-about-such-things mentality and de-cluttering and military-like cleaning operations are scheduled. Despite the burgeoning load, mummy-to-be gets down on her hands and knees and scrubs the skirting boards, silently cursing the years of opportunities she'd had to have done this before without being kicked in the bladder at the same time.

One of two things occurs now. Either a slightly stressful trip to Mothercare is undertaken and items from a 'to buy' list torn out of a magazine are bought without question or histrionics take over. The former is manageable once the bags are returned home and the breast pump instructions have been read (and then re-read), however the latter can bring about a whole new course of action.

The number of people who move house or decide to extend in the last few months of pregnancy is a figure not to be scoffed at. Builders are given deadlines that are in no doubt whatsoever and acquire clients whose patience levels and reasonableness to taking bad news can fluctuate between extremes on an hourly basis. This is without doubt part of the reason why builders are the way they are.

The room is either finished in the nick of time or discussions about babies living in drawers and still becoming fine individuals take place and a child is brought home. Either way, your house is now a family home. And if you're not careful, you have just relinquished all control to the youngest member. Fast forward to present day.

The pink bubble of parenthood has now well and truly burst, leaving an annoying stain on the walls that you've tried to get rid of but still seems to cling on with a life of its own. The children in the house might have outnumbered the adults and the memory of control, order, quiet and anything remotely resembling a lie-in disappeared long ago. Self-esteem is somewhere under a pile of washing, and style, taste and aspirations are clogging up the filter in the dishwasher.

Something breaks the camel's back. The proverbial straw - a trigger, be it large (a party when your house is going to be in full view of people who you think are more in control of their lives than you are of yours) or a just a general final act of destruction from a small creature that sends you through the roof. The house needs to be sorted and the desire to work it out immediately, no hesitation, no questions asked, erupts in a flurry of magazine purchases and discussions over the phone with your mother. She understands, of course she does, but how about those closer to home?

'Thinking Space' is the first space in 'Family Thinking' and is the essence of this foundation. To create a home that works collaboratively, efficiently, calmly and sanely, you need to understand how everyone else thinks. It's time to merge together your strengths and balance out your weaknesses. This space is about figuring out how other people think and behave and being able to accommodate their varying styles (and then with a bucket load of patience and the persuasive skills of a good girl at Christmas, you'll teach your family how to reciprocate such generosity and kindness).

Why do you need to consider other people?

Now, you might be lucky enough to live with someone who wouldn't recognise style if it slapped them round the face with a wet fish and is happy to let you make all the decisions, in which case all the hard work you undertook in the Me Space chapter will now pay off big time as you will have the joy of surrounding yourself with all the patterns, textures, colours and shapes that truly reflect who you are and what you want to say to the world.

However, it's more than likely that another pair of eyes will be used to, at best, glance over the purchases before declaring a final yay or nay. And even if you're in the hallowed position of this only being a financial decision then sooner or later you will begin to realise that this isn't just about decorative taste and whether you like the

Bohemian look or are more partial to Neo-classical ornamentation. You will soon discover that designing involves considering the functional needs of the home as much as the aesthetic.

Function

Who sleeps where and how, who cooks, who leaves the house first, who talks and spends time with whom in which room, who needs über-efficient storage, who needs hours in the bathroom, who knows where the Dyson is kept? So the input of your partner, minimal though it may be, cannot be ignored all together. You have to understand his movements, habits and methods even if he's not really bothered by the colour of the walls he's living between.

There are also children to bear in mind. Soon enough they will have an opinion on how their rooms look, not to mention the rest of the house (depending on how creative your children are). If you want to encourage this creativity, it's an interesting experiment to involve them in certain decisions, namely what colours they would like in their bedroom. (Then it's down to your skills of negotiation and influence to make sure the room doesn't end up looking like Barbie's house by encouraging a modicum of balance to the scheme.)

Thinking Space is about understanding what others want from their home and seamlessly fusing it with your own now very well-developed sense of what home means to you. Where Me Space was all about me, me, me (and by that I mean you, you, you), Thinking Space, is about we, we, we (not the Wii, it might be worth noting).

Is that even possible, you may be asking? Can a family live in harmony, in a well-designed, aesthetically pleasing, calm and sane home? I believe so. Perhaps thinking about it differently might help. What will happen if you give up on harmony, good design, pleasing aesthetics, sanity and happiness? What future lies in that direction?

Reality check

We live in stressful times. Phones bleep at us all day long, laptops are constantly on, work hours are insane and the JFDI mentality drives a lot of us to indeed Just (expletive removed for the family audience) Do It, without regard to the consequences on our health or the bigger picture. As we have discussed, children have their own set of demands, which don't come with a rota or allocated time off and as a result the world seems to be making constant demands on our attention and our minds. We try and switch off with a gentle game of Golden Eye on the Wii and find ourselves more wound up than when we started. Or we try and juggle the whole lot, phone calls, while cooking, while feeding the baby, while tweeting and that brings about a similar result of feeling we've been dodging bullets.

Going back to basics and living for a while without technological interruptions is not a reality for most of us. The occasional week camping will, of course, do huge amounts for your well-being and sanity (especially with the reassurance of GPS and the mobile) but camping isn't the answer in the long run. There are more and more TV programmes talking about escaping to the country and we watch in awe at the idea of a simpler life but the likelihood is we'll have been doing so while updating various statuses, changing a nappy or at least texting at the same time. We have actually forgotten what the simple life is.

Believe me, unless that's your thing, (and you should know for sure now, whether it is) I'm not expecting you to go all 'Good Life' on me and start rearing chickens and knitting your children's school uniform. In fact, I'm not even really into 'the simple life' but what I do appreciate is that this hectic life is taking its toll on us, and if we don't balance out the lunacy that is life then we will not be fit to do everything that we want to do in the future. We have to consider how long we can keep this up for.

An answer?

Home is the answer. (Or if it's not THE then at least it's AN answer.) Home is our inner sanctum. It is our escape. It is where we return to every night, where we seek shelter and solace but also where we connect with the most important people in our lives. Our home has to look after us if we want to continue living at the pace we have chosen.

And this requires understanding not only what suits us but also what our partners and the rest of our family need in their inner sancta too. It's all very well having worked out that your personal sanctuary is papered ceiling to floor in 60s style orange and purple flowers but there are others who might just disagree with you. And while I spent most of 'Me Space' pointing out that a bit of self-indulgence from time to time is absolutely vital, it isn't necessarily advisable, or practical, as a constant answer. Flexibility is key when it comes to the family home.

On the other hand, compromise is a dangerous thing and going for the lowest common denominator is not the answer when it comes to decorating your home. Finding something that neither of you hates but equally neither of you has the smallest token of appreciation for, will only lead to a bland home and a bland life. And while I have spelt out quite clearly the perils of hectic living, bland living is not the solution either. Bland living means giving up, bland living means cheerio to personality and adios to opinion, and accepting bland living is the beginning of a downhill journey. And you deserve more than that.

When I say bland, I'm not talking about neutrals and relaxed environments and colours that don't pop out and scream at you. I'm talking about areas of nothingness. When you walk into a room and feel more inclined to walk out again for fear of becoming as boring as the furniture. That is no way to live. It says too much about you. And this is what your kids will grow up thinking is what defines 'home'. As I said, compromise and bland are dangerous.

It's time to understand what you want to say about yourself. What you want to project to others, what you want your children to believe in and what home you want to create for your future and your family.

Lamely handing over the reins of opinion to another is not the solution but neither is battling over whose style is better than whose. Pointing fingers of bad taste at one another is only funny for a while (even if temporarily it's side splittingly hilarious and makes your brain hurt) because soon you have to respect the fact that other people under your roof have been brought up in different places, with different ways of thinking, with varying levels of financial backing and a unique appreciation of culture (or lack thereof) along with it. So once you've stopped laughing at each other, it's time to sit down and work out whether your taste is truly mutually exclusive or whether there's just the most glorious little cross over where you will both be delighted and fulfilled and aesthetically satiated. And the house will look good too. But where do we begin? How do you work out how to make your interior design taste compatible with everyone else's in the family?

Jumping in at the deep end and taking your family on a day trip to Chelsea Harbour (or John Lewis) to look at fabrics and wallpaper is not the solution here. If it were the solution, you would have done it long ago. The likelihood is that you are going to have to try and get this one past with a bit of cunning. And the one way to do this is to find out *how* your partner thinks.

Case study

Mike and Jen had been living together for seven years when they decided to extend their home. They had one child already who had been a very easy baby. Jen was pregnant with their second and they had no reason to believe that this new baby would be any different. It seemed the perfect time to renovate the house – Jen was off work and Mike could spend some of his paternity leave helping out too.

When I met them, the reality had been somewhat different to their plans. Unfortunately there had been a number of complications in the build, which also coincided with severe colic. By the time they were trying to make interior design decisions, neither partner had the patience or the tolerance to accept the other's 'terrible taste' and 'offensive choices'.

I soon discovered that Jen was the creative in the partnership. She was extremely visual and had a real flair for colour. On the other hand Mike was much more interested in keeping things neutral but he wanted texture – (he didn't use that word exactly, he just said it had to 'feel right').

Unfortunately they had been talking at loggerheads and the lack of sleep and the stress involved in the unexpected costs had meant that the patience they normally showed one another just didn't exist.

I explained to them the different ways of thinking (*as described in the following pages*). At first they were somewhat sceptical but as they started to recognise and most importantly, appreciate their differences, their relationship changed. It became more tolerant and understanding and we were able to develop and design them a number of beautiful rooms that truly reflected their personalities as well as incorporating their needs as a growing family.

Now while understanding thinking will not give you eight hours of sleep a night nor will it make you suddenly like the lurid pink paper that your partner thinks is right for the nursery, it will give you the tools to be able to discuss your choices reasonably with your partner and come from a place of respect.

Do you respect/ tolerate/ laugh at/ encourage your partner's style choices?

Thinking types

There are many different methods and tools to determine a person's thinking style or personality type. The Greeks split us into 'humours' - choleric, sanguine, phlegmatic and melancholic - which all sound highly contagious and nothing I'd want to be classed under. Jung looked at our extravert and introvert nature, which I'm sure you've already gathered about your family members and while it is useful to know, it isn't the answer to their interior design needs. Myers Briggs developed on from Jung using the introvert/ extrovert spectrum as one of four in its analyses. It also looks where people sit on the thinking to feeling spectrum, the sensing to intuition spectrum and the judging to perceiving spectrum, leaving you in one of sixteen boxes with some letters attached. It's enjoyable to work out if you're into personality analysis but more for the HR department than family, unless you want to make copious notes and have a reminder card for each child.

The big five aspects of personality are openness, conscientiousness, agreeableness, extraversion and neuroticism. (Obviously some of those sound more appealing than others.) There are tests that are available online for you to assess yourself but again, for the sake of the home, I would recommend simplicity over complexity. This is a place to start rather than a leadership assessment for a promotion. That being said, this overview will give you the basis to work from and if you want to delve a little deeper there is no harm in that at all. However for the time being, let's keep it easy because we've already got too much to do and our aim is to make life easy here, not "more stuff I didn't quite get round to finishing off."

The Dwell-Being personality test

1. Are you more easy-going or dominant?
2. Pick one and grade yourself out of 5 for that one only.
3. Are you more formal or informal?
4. Pick one and grade yourself out of 5.
5. You should have two numbers. Plot your position on the chart:

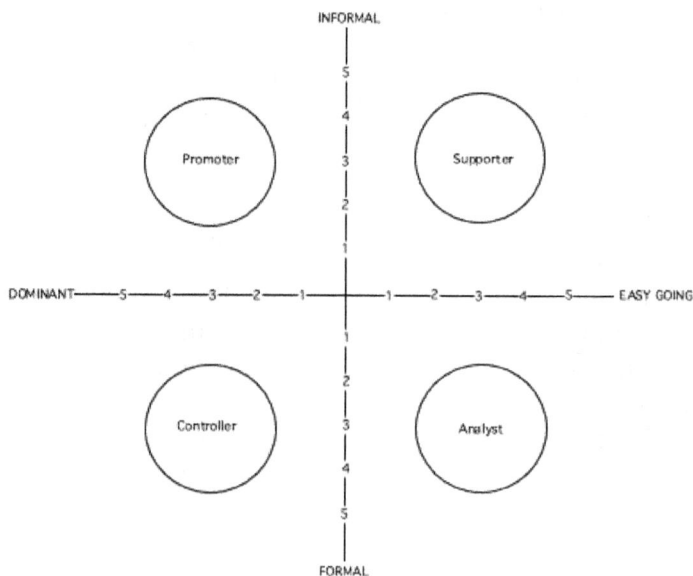

Hopefully you have found yourself in one of the quadrants. For example, if you're easy going (4) and quite informal (2) then you're a 'supporter'. If you're informal (3) but quite dominant (4), you're a 'promoter', etc. These define your style of thinking.

It should be easy to assess yourself and the other grown-up members of your family.

What you can learn about each thinking type:

- What their ideal environment is.
- How they best use their time.
- What their most comfortable pace is.
- What type of information they appreciate.
- What to do to win their acceptance.
- What problem-solving support to provide.
- How to make decisions and how to make it easier for them.

Which type are you?

Supporters

- Work and live best in cooperative, deliberate and friendly environments.
- Develop relationships first before progressing cooperatively.
- Work in a deliberate, steady manner.
- Like to understand why people do things and enjoy the 'just like me' feeling of commonality.
- Appreciate being supported as well as supporting others and make the most of personal attention, particularly when facing problems.
- Make decisions taking as little risk as possible and assess the situation deliberately.
- Are helped by offering opinions, personal assurances and guarantees.

Analysts

- Work and live best in serious, business-like, structured and cooperative environments.
- Use their time thoroughly and organise efficiently.
- Work in a deliberate, steady and orderly manner.
- Listen for documented facts.
- Appreciate the expertise of others and cooperation from others.
- Are helped when the risk is minimised and the answers are rational.
- Make decisions once the facts have been reviewed, the risks minimised and the responsibility has been shared.

Controllers

- Work and live best in a business-like and independent environment.
- Are task-oriented and like to feel in control.
- Work efficiently, effectively and are always directed at end results.
- Work at a fast, efficient pace.
- Like people who are competent, task-oriented and driven.
- Appreciate being given control.
- Solve problems by taking on responsibility and like others to support conclusions and actions.
- Make decisions with speed and logic.

- Are helped to make decisions by providing options with probabilities.

Promoter

- Work and live best in an open climate of support, creativity and thinking.
- Use their time flexibly and openly, and like to first establish a relationship.
- Work at a fast pace.
- Expect to know who you are, what you think and which direction to take.
- Dislike restraints.
- Appreciate recognition and admiration for work well done.
- Like to have their actions, opinions and dreams supported on a personal basis.
- Frequently make decisions emotionally.
- Will make decisions faster with incentive or testimonial.

Making sense of the analysis

Can you see now why, if your partner is an analyst they have no desire to be taken to the high street and let loose making willy-nilly decisions about curtains and wallpaper? Equally if your husband is a promoter he won't want to laboriously gather every catalogue for every door handle type and make a decision once the data has been tabulated formally.

Understanding your partner's thinking type can make life considerably easier if put to good use. Although simple, this tool can give you the basis for a deeper appreciation of how other people approach life. Sometimes just knowing that other people think in a different way to you is enough to change how you handle your relationship with them. Sometimes understanding one single dimension, for example appreciating their ideal pace of work, will have an impact. If you like to work at a hundred miles an hour and have been frustrated until now that your partner takes things slowly, how do you feel about that now? Or perhaps you've always wondered why your partner needs to chat with everyone, why do they need to know the checkout girl's life story before buying the shopping? Can you see why it's important to them now? And can you now tell how some people will make emotional decisions about shopping for goods ('just because...'), whereas others need to have documented facts about why goods should be bought. The interpretations are endless and very useful if you step out of the 'heated debate' and look at the situation rationally.

Homework

What is your style? What is your partner's? Spend some time writing out the ways you would like to be treated and you think your partner would like to be treated in a discussion. Writing it down yourself will make a difference. It's not difficult to understand intellectually and after reading it, I'm sure you've 'got it'. However, it's not until you write it down again or practise it specifically that it will 'sink in'.

Niki Schäfer

The Dwell-Being design process

With a new understanding of how we, and our partners, operate let's have a brief look at the design process and see how each stage is likely to be approached by the different thinking styles. I will go into the design process in more depth in the following chapters, but this overview is a good opportunity to see how the process can be shared out among different thinkers.

Designing is a combination of being creative and also being practical. It requires the ability to switch from one mindset (or head space) to the other. Combining both at the same time will lead to spectacularly average results, so I would recommend that you have faith in the process and allow yourself to indulge in each stage. Or, as we will discuss shortly, find someone who enjoys revelling in that specific way of thinking.

These are the steps involved in the design process – can you think which personality type would be best suited for each phase?

Step 1 – Brainstorming design ideas

Brainstorming is a chance to explore the creative possibilities available, to think outside the box and get a feel for what you like. This requires 'blue sky thinking' where the sky is the limit. Don't hold back with anything as tedious as a practical consideration. Just dream. Let go of the 'what ifs' and the 'oh-no-you-cant's' ricocheting around your head. Simply gather everything you've ever adored or just admired and put it together in a pile. Love that pile. Love the potential that pile can bring. There's the gem of an idea hidden in that pile. And without doubt a load of rubbish ideas too but that's good, that's what brainstorming does, it brings out the good and the bad – allow for both. Feel secure in the knowledge that bad ideas have to come out too, because without them how do you know what the good ideas look like?

Examples of brainstorming
- Mind mapping – start in the centre of a large piece of paper and create a central thought. ('Home' perhaps). From there, pull out bubbles of thought and continue to do so from each thought. Some will link together, and others will be in a world of their own. The idea is that the thinking doesn't have to be linear. Mind mapping is a great way to get lots of thoughts down without having to order them (yet).
- Concept and vision board – this is what we have done with the collection of images. You can also add textures (feathers, shells, a piece of rope), quotes, photos, and paintings. Add any visual element you like to create a board you love. Again, it needn't 'make sense' it just has to be the feeling of what you want to achieve. You have to love it.
- Group discussion – talking helps. Sharing creative ideas often requires images to make sure everyone is on the same page, but talking through how you want to feel in your home is key. It's important to include everyone in your discussion. Children love to be included (especially about

their rooms) and even guests enjoy being asked about how you can meet their needs.

Step 2 – Plotting needs

Put a sensible hat back on (are you the sensible one?) and talk through the basic needs and requirements of the design. Where do the boundaries lie? These can be physical constraints i.e. the size of the house or the plot, or financial ones i.e. the size of the budget. Itemise all the requirements very logically. Make a bullet point for all the different spaces that are required. Example:

- Sleeping
- Eating
- Entertaining
- Playing
- Relaxing etc.

And then list out what is needed in each of these 'zones'.

For example – sleeping

- Bed
- 2 x bedside tables
- Chest of drawers
- Wardrobe
- Dressing table & stool
- Lighting – architectural, wall, pendants, lamps
- Flooring and rugs
- Curtains/ Voiles
- En-suite (if you're lucky)

- Dressing room (if you're blessed)

It sounds basic (because it is) but that doesn't mean it isn't absolutely vital. If you don't write down what you want, you might just oversee it and in a year's time, you'll realise you didn't think very clearly about the boot room and now the whole house is covered in mud. Write it down.

Step 3 – Creating

This is the messy bit (which of you loves getting messy?) It's time to squeeze the ideas from the brainstorm stage into the plot stage. Don't get too hung up on having perfect answers just yet. You still need to think loosely and freely. Have a dabble - move some walls around, see what the bed would feel like in the middle of the bedroom, consider a sunken pit in the garden. Allow your creative mind to come up with some, shall we say, off-the-wall solutions. *(I will take you through examples of this in the next chapter, Dream Space).*

Just giving ideas breathing space is enough to kill some of them off (glass stairs – what with three kids under five and elderly parents?) but others will grow beautifully with the added oxygen (definitely knock that wall through and create a proper-sized room for a teenager).

Obvious ideas come easily, but allowing yourself to experiment will bring about some unexpected results that could become the essence of the house if you let them. This requires creative thinking and some room to breathe. (We'll get on to breathing space shortly.)

Step 4 – Making amendments

Pare your ideas down to three. One of them will be the obvious, one will be the 'out-there' version and one will be a combination of the two. Having a choice between three gives you a more rounded understanding of your options and is why it is advisable to get three quotes (from builders and other trades) so you have a really good comprehension of what the experts make of the job.

Don't rush at making changes - live with your three solutions for a while. Let your brain cogitate over them. Leave them alone and go and do something else for a while. Becoming myopic about the design solution will suffocate the creativity. Let go of the ideas for a while and then return. The answer will be obvious.

Step 5 - Realisation

This is where the devil plays with his/ her (don't want to be sexist) favourite toy – the detail. The realisation process requires accuracy, patience and a love of Excel. Spreadsheets and to do lists central. (So who is the neat freak?)

a. Itemisation – fill out from the bullet points you made in the 'plot' section. Go through every aspect of the room and think about what you need. Walls – paint/ wallpaper. Woodwork – paint. Windows – blinds/ curtains/ shutters.   Floor   – wood/ carpet/ rugs. Lighting – pendant, wall, architectural. Furniture – bed, bedside tables etc. Be thorough. Be boring. This will become your shopping list or your beg/ borrow/ steal list (depending on your budget). It will become a very neat checklist for you later. Do it now when your brain is clear, before the weeks of dust and disruption have settled in.

b. Budget – I am always delighted to find clients who know how much money they have to spend, but they're a rare breed. Most people have no knowledge of how much an armchair costs (£250-£5,000) or what they want to spend on a bed. And because I can source beds at £99 and equally ones that cost over £12,000 and I have no judgement whatsoever about which you choose, it's simply best for me to know a budget so I can get to work and find something appropriate. It's the same for you. One thing's for sure though, if you set off on this process without a figure in mind, you'll spend a lot more than if you do. Guaranteed. You have been warned.

c. Trade – get a little black book. Ask your friends for anyone good they've ever worked with and make a note. Make a concerted effort to visit everyone who has had work done on their home of late and then grill them for all the juicy details. I can assure you, people love to share their tales of woe and equally the bargains and the gems of a tradesperson they found. Re-designing your home is an epic adventure and the idea of not talking about it is a travesty. People will cough up some good stuff for you, if you ask nicely. On the other hand, if you have no friends (or you've just moved to town) then the local trade supply shop will have recommendations. Ask them for tradespeople who have a constant stream of work (a sure indicator that they're good, or, at worst, experienced.)

d. Placing orders – mistakes can be easily made, the wrong product code is all it takes. Errors can be expensive and time-consuming and definitely add unnecessarily to the stress factor. Painstaking accuracy is required here. Triple check your measurements. Go over codes. Get people to read things back to you. And keep everything in writing. Everything. Do not place orders over the phone. You will regret it. Write orders. They take more time, yes, but in a few weeks when someone is questioning what you asked for, you will feel safe in the knowledge that you have a piece of paper filed somewhere (preferably in that room's file) with the purchase order in all its glorious detail. Who loves details?

e. Schedule – again it's time to knuckle down and get some solid figures attached to this part of the realisation process. Ask everyone how long things will take. Ask as many questions as you can. What can go wrong? What are the lead times on that? (Especially glass – it's renowned for being late.) What needs to be in place before you can do this? Collect all the data first and then create a flow chart. Starting at the end can help, I find. Work backwards from where you want to be. Finished room, furniture delivery, curtains hung, second fix lighting/ electrics, carpet laid, install new radiators, paint and decoration, first fix lighting/ electrics, plaster work, carpet removal, radiator removal and plumbing, store furniture to be re-used. (An example of a room not requiring any walls being built.) Keep on top of schedules. They have to be flexible. Being rigid with them will lead to inevitable heart attack. So let them give and take (but don't take any nonsense from your trade, don't let them push you around, don't let them not show up. Be firm but fair. Like a parent.)

Step 6 - Enjoy

This is a stage that frequently goes without mention. However, I think it's important to remind yourself of why you are doing this. You're going to need something to get you through some of the more testing moments in the process, so it's important to have a store of feel good factors in your pocket ready for those occasions. Remind yourself of how great it's going to be. Equally, the process of designing your own home is one people dream about for years beforehand, so it's important that when the dream becomes reality you are able to recognise that this is what you've been planning and plotting all that time. This is it! Enjoy yourself. And most of all enjoy the end product. Have ceremonies along the way to celebrate key milestones (the completion of the roof is a traditional party pit stop) but it could be the bed making it into the room (celebrate as you see fit...). Who is the party person in your relationship?

This is by no means a thorough list of everything that needs to be done (we will be covering the process in more detail over the next chapters), there were no planning applications mentioned, minimal project management, nothing at all about handling day-to-day life with the chaos of refurbishment going on and only a hint at the idea of negotiation. The aim, however, was to break down the process into job types so that now you have a good understanding of how you and your partner think, you can approach each job accordingly.

If you are a promoter and he is an analyst then it is more likely that you will enjoy the brainstorming element more then he will. You can creatively gather as much as possible and then give him the job of working out the parameters. He can be the realist, the fact finder, and the one who calculates the budget and you can be the inspiration.

If you are a supporter and he is a controller then it would be sensible to get him to talk to the trade first. Once they have established what needs to be done and how much time they have to do it in, then you can use your social skills to make sure it gets done in a friendly, happy, as well as efficient, manner. Good workmanship comes from fulfilled workers, not only ones who have strict deadlines.

If you are the analyst, you will revel in the realisation phase and have the whole system under control with impeccable accuracy. This is important. However, if you are not an analyst and nor is your partner, you're more big-thinker types, then you will have to work out who is going to do the precision work. Is it worth getting someone to do it for you?

These are the benefits of having determined your thinking style. It gives you foresight. It enables you to predict how things will be handled, where things are likely to go wrong, and to decide if they are being dealt with by the wrong person. We all think there are some jobs that no one wants to do but it's not true, someone somewhere is motivated to do that job. It's just your job to find that person or find that motivation!

I hope you have a much better understanding of how you and your partner now operate. Do you think differently? Of course you do. Can you appreciate one another for that? Well that's up to you, but it's worth considering, not only for projects but on a day-to-day basis too. (Which type of thinker leaves the loo seat up? It's a fair question...).

Case study

In the past I have had clients who ask only for design ideas and advice but who are willing to see the work through themselves. Beatrice and Sam were a couple whose children had left home and were building their dream home. Sam had never been keen to get advice from someone else but Beatrice wanted someone to talk things through and to get the occasional dose of reassurance.

Having met them several times, I assessed Beatrice to be a supporter and Sam to be a controller. She wanted to share ideas whereas he wanted to control them. She wanted reassurance whereas he knew his own mind very clearly. It became apparent, however, quite soon into the interior process that he had no interest in the softer aspect of the home (the soft furnishings, the colour etc.) however he was very keen to keep an eye on the budget and the structural work. Whenever Beatrice asked him about her part of the job, Sam would always say how busy he was, that he couldn't think about it right now or that it really didn't matter. Until the subject of money came along and he would want to know in minute detail what cost what.

An impasse was reached when they recognised that work was not progressing in the interiors and Beatrice called me to talk things though. We needed a plan to talk to her husband.

As a designer, I could have suggested just taking over and making things easy for both of them, but I didn't think this would resolve the situation. We needed them both to feel comfortable. In truth it wasn't very complicated – on one hand Sam needed to feel in control and on the other Beatrice didn't want the control. To her it felt too much like responsibility and meant making decisions. We needed Sam to take on board the control without feeling that he was being bothered with matters that weren't of interest.

And so I helped her set up business meetings with her husband. We asked Sam to give us a time when he would be ready to briefly look over the choices that had been made, we gave him two options to choose from (on a couple of items only so that he felt involved without being inundated) and we produced a spreadsheet that he could 'sign off'. He felt like the director he had been at work and had the control back and she got the choices and the reassurance without feeling like she had to make the final decision.

Look at your relationship objectively now. Who is the key decision maker?

Children

Working out how children think is a different game altogether. For adults, we can categorise thinking styles along spectrums of formality/informality and dominant/easy-going. These traits are not yet fully developed enough in children to be an effective way of understanding them, and while you may be able to have a guess at their level of formality ("No Mummy, I think a tie for dinner would be best") and their dominant stance in life, it's not as developed as it could be.

It's important to understand how our children approach their world. We often assume our kids are just mini versions of us and while in many respects they are, they also have their own attitudes and opinions. They think differently to us and learning to appreciate that will have a significant effect on your relationship with them. It is this level of understanding that will bring calmness and sanity into your home.

Do you want to really know what's going on in your kids' heads? Can you imagine how much easier life would be if you could understand not only what they are doing but why they are doing it? NLP can help. (I'd go as far as to call it magic, but there are probably laws and clauses restricting such words, so we'll just call it 'jolly useful stuff', shall we?)

How do your children think?

In NLP (Neuro Linguistic Programming – the study of how we think and how to improve our ways of thinking) there is a method of determining thinking style that will help you understand your child's approach to the world.

A quick lesson in NLP

Our view of the world is determined by our senses – we see, we hear, we feel, we taste, we smell and we make sense of. We take any experience and we represent it to ourselves internally (i.e. in our brain) through our senses:

- Visual (sight)
- Auditory (hearing)
- Kinaesthetic (touch)
- Gustatory (taste)
- Olfactory (smell)
- Auditory digital (logically)

To begin with (as babies) we experience everything using all five senses (this explains why little ones put objects into their mouths - they are using their gustatory system to understand their world) but as we grow up we focus on the senses that are most effective (most of us giving up the gustatory, it being considered impolite to chew on new people or objects as we once did).

Children are sponges of learning and from birth (and before) are making connections with feelings, words, actions and symbols – they quickly learn to focus on what's most effective. If I scream, that nice lady over there will bring me some food. If I smile, that funny man will pay me some attention. They use all their senses to learn – if I throw the toy on the floor, will someone pick it up? If I touch that will it feel soft/ be prickly/ be heavy/ burn me? Some learn faster than others.

Lead representational system

While we use all five of our senses, some are relied upon more heavily than others. We learn to favour one way over the others and there is soon one system that leads the thought. This is called the lead representational system.

Working out which way you and your child think is an invaluable way of being able to understand how they see, hear or feel the world and will make sense of all kinds of areas when you discover that you all think differently.

This is what our senses look and feel like on the outside and the inside:

Visual – means looking outside and mentally visualising.
- Do you think in pictures and movies?
- Think of your living room. Now change the walls to bright purple.
- Was that easy to do?

Auditory – hearing external sounds and recalling internal

sounds.
- Do you rehear conversations easily?
- Can you hear people's voices with distinct clarity?
- Can you mimic accents well? (By 'eck Ma...)

Kinaesthetic – refers to sensations of touch, temperature and texture. Bodily awareness (e.g. balance) is also part of this - some of us remember how to move and hold our bodies more easily than others.
- Do you remember emotions and how you felt easily?
- Can you stand on one leg and close your eyes without falling over?

Olfactory – refers to sensations of smell.
- Can the smell of an old hairspray bring about strong memories?

Gustatory – is how we handle the sensations of taste.
- Do you have apple crumble and custard inspired memories?

Visual

A visual child will be very observant, will notice small details and changes that have been made – if you've cut your hair, if the fence has been painted. They will enjoy watching people and seeing how different we all are. They like visual hobbies and will also be very protective of their artwork and upset if it is ruined (or accidentally found in the bin, shame on me...). They will enjoy making decisions about what to wear. They also have a great visual memory and frequently know where things are – your car keys, their other ballet slipper. They will definitely have a say in how they want their room to look.

Auditory

Children who are auditory might be sensitive to noise and cover their ears if a fire engine screeches by, for example. They can find it difficult to concentrate in a noisy room and will tell people off for talking when the TV is on. They love to chat and will often talk to themselves and their teddy bears when left alone. They love to sing and can remember words to songs and nursery rhymes with ease.

Kinaesthetic

A child who is led by feeling will love physical contact and be the supplier of fine cuddles. They won't hang around for long though as they find it hard to sit still. They tend to enjoy sport, individual or team, as long as they are in movement. This need to move is on-going and it can be difficult for them to sit still in class. You might notice that they pace or fidget when you are talking to them about something important (be patient, it's just how they are processing their thoughts). Kinaesthetic children can also be sensitive to how things feel on them. They're the ones who refuse to wear the itchy woollen scarf and complain endlessly about the label.

Olfactory and gustatory (smell and taste) are rare lead systems and are frequently bracketed under the kinaesthetic system. There is another system, however, which is a result of how we have compiled the data from the other systems – it is the language of our own understanding and is called the auditory digital system.

Auditory digital

A child who is led by their auditory digital system is a curious child, the endless 'why' questions that take place at two years will continue throughout childhood. They want to know how things work and what everything means. They like order in their lives and will have special places for all their toys, which they will group with care. You might find all their cars lined neatly at the end of play. This organisation works in their planning and they will often have thought things through – who will be sitting where in the car, how many car seats are needed. They also enjoy comparing and discovering what makes the best and what their favourite anything is (breakfast cereal, friend, playgroup). They might also compare what they receive with regard to their siblings. ("But Mummy, he had a friend over last week and the week before and I haven't had my friends here for ages.")

Homework (part 1)

Ask your child to bring you, or show you, their favourite part of their bedroom. Does it fit with the way of thinking you suspect them to have? Has the kinaesthetic brought you a soft teddy? Did your visual daughter show you the colour of her walls or the funky cushion cover? Did your auditory son tell you about how he adores his iPod? Did the auditory digital child proudly show off their neat shelves and labelled boxes?

If you are changing the children's rooms, consider how best they can let you know what they want from their room – a concept board, (like the one you have created) or just a safe discussion while you're wrapped up in bed one Sunday morning. And if your child is auditory digital then consider giving them a list of items for them to choose from and organise.

Do one of these things. You'll be surprised at how your children will actually help you (and enjoy doing it!).

Obviously it's incredibly important that you actually pay attention to their answers. If they produce a beautiful concept board for you then let this be the inspiration for their room (I'll teach you how in the next chapters) and if they bring you fluffy cushions and talk about how they love the feel of their cupboard handles, then make sure you incorporate these texture based elements into their new room.

Homework (part 2)

You will recognise where your child fits in these categories I'm sure, but how about you? Sometimes it is difficult to recognise ourselves with such clarity. Try the following test to discover your own way of thinking:

Score each of the following phrases as follows:
1. Least describes you
2. Better
3. Better still
4. Describes you best

I have a morning to myself and decide to relax at home. I relax when:

a) (....) I feel the comfort of the sofa and cushions and the warmth of the fire.

b) (....) I notice how quiet everything is or can appreciate my own music.

c) (....) I smile at the happy photos on the mantel and artwork on the fridge, I see my home without the distractions of others.

d) (....) I know this makes sense, I've worked all week long and I deserve this rest time.

I have an argument with a good friend and am most affected by:

a) (...) My friend's tone of voice and the words she uses.

b) (...) How logical or illogical the discussion is.

c) (...) My friend's true feelings and how they feel to me.

d)(...) My friend's point of view and how she sees the situation.

I am helping out at an event, I prefer:

a) (...) To be told what is going to happen, when and where.

b) (...) To get a picture of what I think is necessary.

c) (...) To feel out how things will run.

d) (...) To understand what makes sense of the job.

I attend a presentation and find it easy to follow because:

a) (...) The charts are clear and the displays are colourful

b) (...) The presentation is factual and the thinking makes sense.

c) (...) The presenter speaks clearly and sets the right tone for the evening.

d) (...) I have a real feeling for the subject and can grasp the presenter's points easily.

I have lots of work to do and am overwhelmed because:
a) (....) I can't see the wood for the trees.
b) (....) I'm out of my depth.
c) (....) I can't process what needs to happen next.
d) (....) I'm not tuned into what to do.
I've been working something out with my partner and he says something I really agree with and I say:
a) (....) Yes, that feels right.
b) (....) Yes, that sounds right.
c) (....) Yes, that looks right.
d) (....) Yes, that makes sense.

I'm organising a family party, I work out how well I am doing based on:
a) (....) My comprehension of the tasks required.
b) (....) How I see the event happening.
c) (....) What other people are saying to me.
d) (....) How I feel about the event.

One of my strong points is my ability to:
a) (....) Tune into what's happening.
b) (....) See answers clearly.
c) (....) Get in touch with how I feel.
d) (....) Make sense of the situation.

Make a note of the points you allocated to each statement in the box below. For question 1 – how many points did you give statement c)? Put this number in the first box. How many points did you give statement b)? Put this in

the second box. And so on. Add up the points to a total at
the bottom.

Question	Visual	Auditory	Kinaesthetic	Auditory Digital
1	c	B	a	d
2	d	a	c	b
3	b	a	c	d
4	a	c	d	b
5	a	d	b	c
6	c	b	a	d
7	b	c	d	a
8	b	a	c	d
TOTAL	V=	A=	K=	Ad=

The totals will show you a relative preference for one of
the four major representational systems. Clearly, there
are no right and wrong answers here. This is just a way
of indicating how your brain is 'wired'. You may have a
clear leading system, a visual approach that you will see
with ease now, as the points are obviously considerably
higher. On the other hand, you might have a more
balanced approach to your thinking and the totals are
more in line with one another. There may be one that just
edges forward though. Whether you have an obvious
'winner' or you are more evenly spread, this will give
you an idea of how you think and importantly will show
you how different you can be from other people –
especially those very close to you.

It is interesting to get your partner to do this exercise too.
Even if you believe you have all the same beliefs and

values in life, you will probably discover you think about them in different ways. And neither of you is more 'right' about the way in which you think about anything, it's just what's right for you.

I found this quite liberating. Probably because I've come from a background where things are right or wrong and there's very little middle ground. So I was really excited to discover there's nothing but middle ground and it's just how I interpret it that will help me feel more 'right' or 'wrong'. Understanding someone else's point of view took on a whole new meaning to me. Learning how to use these observations and understandings and being able to harness them to influence others is a skill worth having.

Obviously you won't be able to sit everyone down and ask them to be assessed with this method even if it is for the greater good. It's just not practical ("Sorry, there'll be a short test before we serve canapés, if you don't mind stepping into the study before you make your way through to the party..."). Luckily, we give clues in the way we think in our choice of language. The words we use every day are a direct reflection of what is going on in our minds.

"I see," says the visually lead person. "That's brilliant. It really shines out from the rest."
"Oh, that's clicked now," says the auditory voice, "the tone is just right and the words really rang a bell."
"I'm touched," says the kinaesthetic, "I've got a really good grasp on how this makes me feel."

"It all makes sense now," says the auditory digital mind, "I understand the process."

Listen carefully to those around you. Their words will give their way of thinking away to you. This takes practice at first but soon you will be able to spot the differences quite quickly and know how best to talk to them. Famous therapists have been known to simply 'translate' from one way of thinking to another to help people get through their problems. They help one party see the issue and another feel better about it. They point out how things are perceived by one but don't resonate with another. And as a result life becomes less foggy and more focussed, or more in harmony, or easier to get a hold of, or simply better understood. Words are such a fabulous window into our minds, we are literally speaking out how we feel to each other and all we have to do is listen carefully.

Using language to your benefit:

For a visual and kinaesthetic couple

If your partner does not feel the need to go shopping for bedroom furniture and you can't see why, then perhaps you can help him get a more solid idea of the project by getting him in touch with what it will ultimately feel like in the room. You can clearly visualise the room but he needs to tap into the way the finished room will make him feel.

For an audio and auditory digital couple

On the other hand, you might be tuned into the whole project beautifully but he just can't make sense of it. You need to help him perceive the benefits of the changes. You need to consider his motivations, let him make sense of the process and let him know the distinct decisions that will need to be made so he can comprehend it all.

This is not an exact science and of course we all use words and speech patterns from every aspect of our thinking but it is useful to have as an overall picture of how you both operate. If you use this to your advantage you will find things moving considerably smoother in your house.

Design implications

A home needs to reflect all of these ways of thinking. While humans need to be flexible in their approach with others ("Let me draw you a picture, my visually led wife, this will explain the off-side rule perfectly"), a house can be designed to accommodate the different types of people who live there.

Visual

Those who have a dominant visual thinking style are likely to be comforted and equally excited by what they see. The choice of colours for these people will be important. Aesthetics on the whole will play a large role in their appreciation of the home. It will have to look the part and show a clear picture of how they see life. The accessories will need to shine out, the art will be vital, the colour palette and the subtleties of how things look in different lights will need to be shown off. A home for these people will very much depend on how it looks. It needs to be outrageously gorgeous!

Auditory

Something as simple as the right doorbell chime will have an impact on auditory thinkers. It will put a smile on their face every time they hear it. A kick-ass music system might also be a wise investment and the ability to control the tunes in each room (including the shower) will give them a real sense of satisfaction. Chimes might work for the less techy and more nature-minded auditory people. Wind hitting the chimes to create a series of notes can be an unpredicted pleasure for these minds.

Kinaesthetic

The use of texture for the feeling folk is incredibly important, especially for children who seek comfort in blankets and soft teddies. Sheepskin rugs, bed throws, Mongolian cushions will be instant winners if you have a kinaesthetic child who previously has been living with linen. Faux fur throws on the sofa are also very successful – it's a lovely sight to see all the children snuggled up under one together.

Textured wallpapers and fabrics are important too, the right feel of a door handle or light-pull will please a kinaesthetic mind. Even the feel under foot is important. Consider the journey from the car to the home – do they like the crunch of the gravel? – does that make them feel at home or would they prefer a smoother trip to the front door?

Activity is also really important for kinaesthetic people. They love to move and, especially for children, who don't have the same liberty of being able to 'just go and play on the street' as we did a few decades ago. They need to release some of their energy. We have a small re-bounder (trampoline) in the house to let off the steam and it's hopefully saved a few ornaments that would otherwise have been broken if my boy had got his hands on the football instead.

Olfactory and gustatory

Fragrance can have a much greater impact on you than you might think. Don't you remember clearly how your school smelt? Or the old people's home you had to go and visit to see you Great Grandmother? And how about the smell of certain foods cooking? These can bring back memories with an alarming rush. So why not harness that and install a fragrance that you would like to be associated with your home? Find a candle or incense or bunch of flowers that will start a memory for your children. It beats burnt toast.

Auditory digital

Organisation and efficiency are paramount for these thinkers. Invest in a designed wardrobe with special drawers for special things. They will be in heaven! The utility room needs to be designed to within an inch of its life. Have hooks with names on, find boxes that fit perfectly on to shelves, code items if you really want to push the boat out.

Cleanliness and order will play key roles too. A cluttered environment will stress an AD brain, while a kinaesthetic will barely notice. Clear floor space, good flow, efficient storage, minimal decoration and even some sense of uniformity will all be appreciated by the auditory digital type.

Can you see now why certain people lose the plot when the house is a mess and another might think they have 'over-reacted somewhat'? Does this explain why some people love colour on every surface but don't really care what it feels like? Do all the household gadgets make sense now? And the music being played from dusk till dawn – is that still so annoying? Of course not, it's simply what people need. And it's our job, as the designer of the home, to be able to understand the needs of the household and then weave in the right elements to suit the appropriate people.

Obviously this doesn't mean that each room must be designed to suit each different thinking type (though that could be an interesting experiment to see who is most comfortable where). The house has to be designed for everyone's use but it is worth understanding that you can have an influence on people, how comfortable they are, how happy they are and most importantly how much they feel 'at home'.

In the next chapter we are going to look at the 'dream space', which will include the bedroom area, a space associated with sharing! It could serve you well to understand how you and your partner think before we progress into actually designing a great room for you.

Homework overview:

The Dwell-Being personality test

- Are you more easy-going or dominant?
- Pick one and grade yourself out of 5.
- Are you more formal or informal?
- Pick one and grade yourself out of 5.
- Plot your position on the chart:

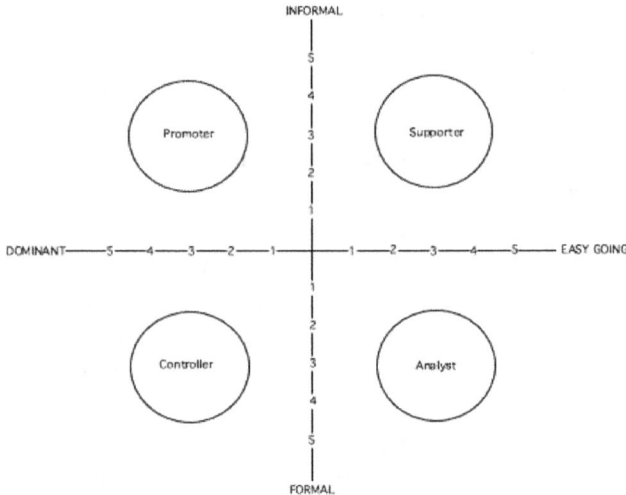

- Understand your type and your partner's.

Representational thinking types – visual, auditory, kinaesthetic, gustatory, olfactory, auditory digital

- Which type are you?
- Which type is your partner?
- Which types are your children?
- What impact do you think this has on your house? Give this some thought. Write it down in your journal (then rush out and buy some furry cushions.)

Congratulations

Even if you don't do a single exercise from this chapter, just by having read it, you will have shifted your perception about the other people who share your home with you. Just being aware that one person thinks differently to another (and they're not doing it just to annoy you) can be truly liberating. It will bring with it a new level of comprehension and as a result, patience. Step by step you *are* changing your life and bringing calmness and sanity into your home.

FOUNDATION 2: FAMILY THINKING

Space 5 - Dream Space

"I have a dream..."
Martin Luther King

"...I have a dream."
ABBA.

DWELL-BEING MODEL

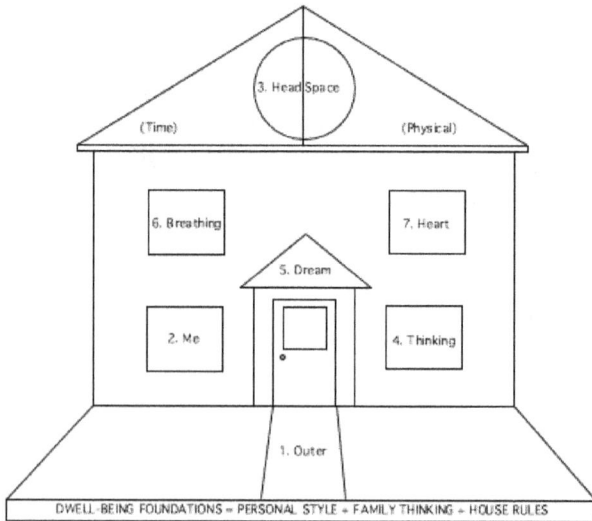

DWELL-BEING FOUNDATIONS = PERSONAL STYLE + FAMILY THINKING + HOUSE RULES

Outer Space
o You've given plenty of thought to what home means to you and realise how everyone's houses are completely different.
o You love your front door and it creates a positive shift in your well-being every time you cross your threshold.

Me Space
o You've torn several magazines up and found huge joy in finding images and photographs that represent who you were, who you are today and who you want to be.

Head Space
o You are well and truly settled into your personal space and the family respects it's just for you.
o You are getting to grips with your 'school timetable' and next week is looking a lot more efficient than last week.

You've built a firm foundation in personal style and have a genuine confidence in what pleases you and what doesn't. Enjoy this sensation and allow it to grow with every design decision you make.

Thinking Space
o You can't believe how obvious it is that you and your husband have such a different approach to shopping. You've also made some really valuable observations about how your children think and are already talking to them differently and handling them better.

These are the spaces you have still to journey through.

Dream Space
o   We will design places to sleep.
o   And make space to envision life as you want it.

Breathing Space
o   We will craft places to relax.
o   And establish space to connect with family and friends and to just 'be'.

Heart Space
o   We will organise places to eat and be together.
o   And build space to feel, to listen, to be heard and to be loved.

Conclusion
o   We will look at housekeeping and house rules - dos and don'ts.
o   And celebrate how confident we feel about the home now.

Dream space chapter outcome

While the last chapter focused on the 'science' of a home (understanding how you both think and then learning some neuroscience strategies to help you make the most of your differences), this chapter is about the art of creating a space that is special for you both.

By the end of this chapter you will:

- Know the design process of a complete room (a process you will be able to repeat time and time again).
- Be privy to the secrets of the 'success formula' that has made millions of millionaires and will also help you to be happy in your home.
- Understand how to create compelling goals and dreams for your own future and feel brave enough to make them happen!

PART I
Dream space

You will need some equipment for later in this chapter.
- Several pieces of graph paper.
- Pencil (HB or harder, not soft black).
- A scale rule (or normal ruler if you are reasonably competent at maths).
- A tape measure.

Designing a bedroom

The bedroom is the most intimate space in the house. It is (generally) shared and must therefore meet the needs of both people living in it. While a living room is more flexible and can therefore be more forgiving, a sleeping space is demanding, because our sleep is so fundamental to our moods and to our health. (Ask a person who doesn't sleep very well... in fact it's probably best that you don't!)

Ordinarily I wouldn't recommend that you start with the master bedroom of the house. I'd start with a far simpler room, a place where you can experiment safely, such as a guest bedroom (or the downstairs loo). So I'll leave it up to you to determine whether you have worked out the styles (both aesthetic and thinking) of you and your partner and feel confident to jump in at the deep end with the master suite or leave it until later.

From a design process perspective, however, there is no difference. You will go through the same stages, which I will break down for you now. From a psychological perspective, however, there are easier places to begin with, as I've already said.

As we saw in the last chapter there are six stages to the design process.
1. Brainstorming
2. Plotting
3. Creating
4. Dwelling
5. Realising
6. Enjoying

You have already completed the brainstorming step (for yourself at least) in the work you completed in Me Space. You've collected a number of images that remind you of who you are, who you were and who you want to be and you have noted the colours, shapes, patterns and influences that please you. You have clearly defined your own style.

Working together (hopefully!)

Did you do this with your partner? The majority of my
clients are either families or couples and it is, for the most
part, the wife who shows me the collection of tear-out
sheets and collated memorabilia. I have a questionnaire
that I like my clients to fill out so I can gain an
understanding of their individual tastes and more often
than not, I need to persuade the male, rather than the
female half of the party, that this is an invaluable part of
the process. So if you have succeeded in getting your
husband's involvement in this initial stage then I
congratulate you.

Brainstorming

Brainstorming consists of gathering your images and
room ideas together, printing things from the Internet,
pooling images, photographs, furniture and lighting
designs to create a visual collection of what you actually
like (as opposed to what will just 'do' or what you're
both willing to 'put up with'). This will enable you to see
how the designs work together.

Once you are pleased with your collection, show the
ideas to your husband in the following order:
1. TV thoughts
2. Audio visual equipment
3. Gadgets – Lutron lighting system etc.
4. Drinks fridge
5. Fabrics

(This is purely my experience speaking. I don't know your husband and he may very well be interested in the fabric selection first. I only want to help you be as influential as possible in getting the right outcome for you both.)

You have an understanding now of what makes him tick and it's up to you to use that knowledge to make the process smooth and happy. And it's amazing what a few well thought through words can have. If he's a visual thinker, talk about the look, if he's kinaesthetic then show him some great handles that he can get a hold of and if he's auditory or auditory digital, then revert to plan A and stick with my initial TV, AV, gadget line up.

Plotting

Plotting requires measuring the site accurately and putting the dimensions on to a technical drawing. I love to plot the layout of a building and work out where everything can fit. However, I have to admit that I enjoy doing this more on an instinctive basis than I do in a precisely measured and defined way. (In truth, I get someone else to do my measuring because I just don't have the mindset to be fastidiously accurate.) I also have to admit that it takes me some considerable time to get into the head space of doing technical drawings. (I find them a bit like swimming – when I'm there it's great but the idea of getting wet and smelling of chlorine never appeals.) Same with technical drawing, when I'm there I'm focused and I find it hugely enjoyable creating layouts and elevations for my clients to understand my ideas clearly. However, honestly, the thought of technical drawings isn't always appealing. So please think carefully about who is going to do the plotting step because it requires accuracy and patience.

Homework

The plan

You will need the graph paper and measuring tape for this step. You are going to measure the bedroom you are designing and create a drawn 'plan' so that you can experiment with some furniture layout options.

Each square on the graph will represent a square area. The size of this will be dependent on the size of the paper you have and the extent of your bedroom. Assuming you are working on an A4 (297x210mm) piece of paper then you need to work out what would be the best size for each square. We can then calculate a scale for the plan.

Most interior plans are either 1:10 for drawing up a single piece of furniture, 1:20 for a small room and 1:50 for an average to large sized room. Most architectural plans are 1:100 or 1:200 and they are printed on to much larger pieces of paper.

However, we are starting simply. So let's assume that your room is a very ample 7m x 5m with a large window overlooking the back garden. For now I'll leave out en-suites and walk-in wardrobes and keep it super simple.

You can easily fit this on to an A4 piece of graph paper, where each blue (darker line) square represents 500mm/ 50cm/ 0.5m squared. Professional interior designers use millimetres so we can be accurate (this is particularly important for furniture design) but they're a bit fiddly and can be mixed up easily to begin with so let's stick with centimetres. This means that each blue square is 50cm x 50cm.

You need to carefully measure each of the wall lengths. Start in one corner and work your way round the outer edges so that you get the perimeter on record.

Then calculate the distance from the wall to the door edge and the width of the door and mark the door on the drawing too. Do the same for the window.

Please keep this simple – measure to the walls (ignore skirting), measure to the door frame (ignore jambs), measure to the aperture – the window opening (ignore where the sill ends). K.I.S.S. (Keep It Simple Schweetie).

Your room drawing may look a little like this.

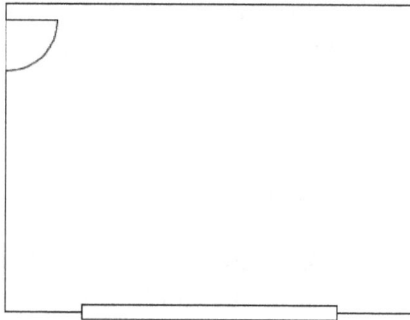

Using another piece of graph paper cut out some furniture templates. Use the same scale 1cm:50cm (because we're going to place them on to the room layout and they need to be measured the same way).

Create the following templates.

Bed (200cm x 200cm) = 4 cm x 4 cm or 4 blue squares x 4 blues squares.

Bedside table (50cm x 50cm) = 1cm x 1cm or 1 blue square x 1 blue square

Do you get the idea?

Add a wardrobe – needs to be 60-75cm deep but width will depend where you put it.

Do you want a dressing table? – They differ but a good size is 140cm x 45cm

And a stool – a circular with a diameter of 40cm.

And what do you want at the end of your bed? A trunk for blankets and winter clothes? Or perhaps a unit with a hydraulic TV built in that you can bring up by the touch of a button?

Create a few objects out of the graph paper, using the correct scale and then start to place them on the layout. Experiment where they may go. Your first solution might look something like this:

If you play around you could achieve a layout that looks like this:

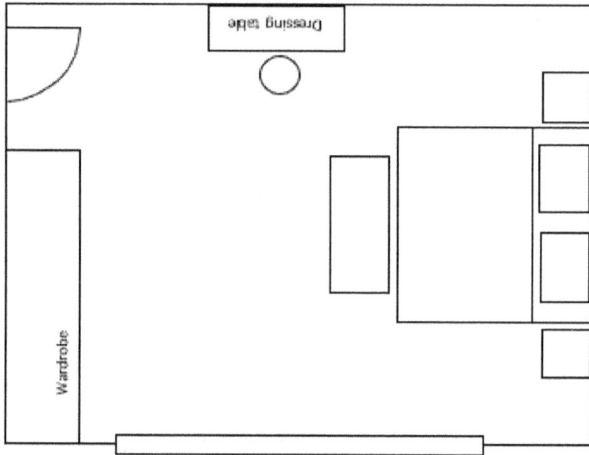

These are two obvious layouts and could work for any bedroom. However, this process is about what works best for you, for your lifestyle and your thinking styles.

Visual considerations

Does your window provide a great view that you can admire while lying in bed? If so, you're more likely to prefer the bed in the first position. If, on the other hand, your bed head is a spectacular piece of craftsmanship or a gorgeous fabric then you'd probably prefer layout 2 so that you can appreciate it fully as you walk into the room.

Here is an alternative bedroom arrangement. This layout works well for smaller rooms, where you still want a dressing area. I've positioned the bed centrally and the dressing table is hidden behind the bed head. In essence we have created a dressing room behind the bed. With further development and an understanding of the house's plumbing this area could become an en-suite bathroom.

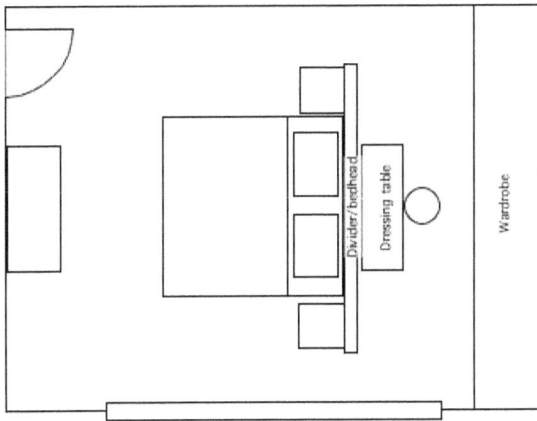

Windows

Please note that there is plenty of space either side of the window for the curtains to be pulled back. This is called 'stack back' and can require quite a considerable amount of space depending on the thickness of your fabrics and the width of the window itself. Allow 20-25% of the width of the window for stack back. For example, if the window is 200cm wide, allow 40-50cm on each side.

The windows I'm using in this example are very simple, but there are many different types of windows and each require some careful thought. Firstly, are they in good condition? How much of a draft is there? You will need to line your bedroom curtains for sure, but if there is a draft then an inter-liner is also a good idea. Perhaps you don't like curtains and would prefer blinds. There is a multitude of blinds solutions and each will depend on your personal style. It's worth having someone measure the window professionally if you are going to be fitting blinds and certainly if shutters are an option. Windows, especially those in older buildings, can be downright wonky and the window treatment needs to be designed around the window – not the other way round. This is particularly relevant for arched windows, portholes and roof windows. For most of these window shapes, there are specialist solutions.

Furniture

In our example, there is also plenty of space for some kind of seating. Do you like a chaise longue in the bedroom? Now your taste is starting to come into play. You might want a small Chesterfield sofa or you might think beanbags are more your style. Only you have the answers. We will go on to discuss how to coordinate your decorative scheme in the next chapter but it's worth bearing in mind that certain decorative choices will have an impact on the layout.

As I've mentioned you might have an incredibly impressive bed head – carved wood, buttoned leather, padded silk squares, pink rubber (who knows...?) - and being able to appreciate that will play a role in your layout decisions. If you have a painting that you love to look at from your bed you'll have to take this into consideration when positioning the bed. You will definitely require storage in your bedroom (unless you have a completely separate dressing room) and your choice of freestanding or fitted furniture will again impact the layout of the room.

Another area to bear in mind is somewhere generally given little thought – the area a door takes to swing. The door swing as you enter any room should be free of corners – be they of imposing wardrobes or the sharper variety that can stab into a hip when you least need it. The door swings of your cupboards also need to be taken into consideration, as it's best to be able to stand in front of a fully opened cupboard door. The same goes for drawers, leave yourself plenty of room to stand in front. Feeling cramped is not a nice sensation and certainly not something you want to do every day, so design that feeling away.

Flow

Ensuring there is flow in your home is incredibly important. Today's shopping habits result in houses that are full to capacity. The attic is jammed, the garage packed, the space under the bed is crammed with boxes. How are we to create space for our belongings?

Do you love to de-clutter or are you a secret hoarder? I really enjoy getting rid of stuff, especially if it's broken or simply not needed any more. It gives me a great sense of satisfaction to either give the better items away or (if I can be bothered) try and sell them in my local newspaper or online. And while it's probably terribly un-PC, I'm also rather fond of the dump. It can be tragic to see so much going to waste but I'm sure there's a network of people who excel in salvage. And that's another thing I love – salvage. One man's junk is another man's treasure and all that. Happy days.

To put it simply, creating flow in your home means you don't walk into things. You don't stub your toe. And as everyone who stubs their toes knows, we only stub our toes when they are cold and particularly sensitive and this means first thing in the morning. And if we stub our toe first thing in the morning we inevitably start the day in a grump. We let the kids know about our moods in no uncertain terms at breakfast and they leave to school feeling like the world isn't fair. They then take this forward to school and either pick on their friends, if they're that way inclined, or sit and mope, if this is more their way of handling being shouted at. They feel sorry for themselves and they pay little attention in class. The teacher notices and humiliates them by pointing out their 'daydreaming' tendencies, thereby exacerbating the situation. Your child returns home after a 'very bad day at school' and is not inclined to help around the house or play nicely with her little brother as a result. The cat might also be kicked.

All of this can be easily resolved. By de-cluttering. We need free space to move around our home comfortably. Everyone needs to feel they have some private space of their own (including you, as we discussed in the first chapter). We need space to work efficiently in a kitchen, we need space to get dressed, we need space to simply slob out on the sofa. We need space to feel good.

Too much space?

Now, if you're in the hallowed position of having a very large home, then it's worth pointing out that space can also be excessive. A void is not what you're looking for. You will feel that too. You may feel strangely lonely or that you can hear yourself think. A cavernous room can be echo-y and this isn't very comforting. People do strange things in spare space – we skate or slide or let out funny noises. Watch your kids next time they're in a large open room.

If you have some spare space, consider now how you could fill it. A beautiful display maybe, a bookshelf of your favourite books, a sculpture, a rocking horse, a chair that looks out of this world but that doesn't have to be remotely comfortable because it's only there for looking at, not sitting on (God forbid!)? Large spaces can also be noisy spaces. If your room has acoustic issues and noise bounces off the walls then think about using fabrics to soften the space. Use upholstered furniture, fabric wall hangings and plenty of curtaining. If you have done your homework well, I'm sure your mind is full of ideas.

This chapter is about creating a dream space for you and your partner. It's about designing a room that will work for you both. I have chosen the bedroom because it is a room that has to work for you both but the principles of measuring and experimenting with layouts will work for all other rooms.

Here are some specific considerations for the bedroom though.

- Who gets up first? Is that for an early train leaving someone else trying to sleep?
- Who reads before they go to sleep? Is that both of you or just the one?
- Who can't sleep in the night and likes to pace?
- Who needs the most wardrobe space?
- Who wants to see all their shoes beautifully lit and on display?
- Who has neat freak tendencies, and who is a bit sloppy round the edges?
- Who takes care of the laundry basket?
- Who leaves their clothes on the floor?
- Who neatly folds their clothes and puts them away every night?
- Who wants to put their makeup on in the bedroom? And is there sufficient natural light to do this?
- Who wants to swing from the chandelier?
- Who wants the feel of soft warm carpet underfoot?

This list is far from conclusive but it opens up the mind to the idea that a bedroom has many functions to play. It is where we sleep but it is also where we dress, where we lie in and read papers, it's where we are intimate and it's where the kids crawl into bed with us at 5.30am.

Take into consideration the needs of your partner and your children as you design your bedroom. I ask you, is a lock a solution?

Case study

Suzie had started her own business 18 months before hand and when I met her she was juggling balls like crazy, multi-tasking galore, trying to do everything at once, taking very little care of herself and not sleeping very well.

My intention had been to help her with some time management and organisation but, as is often the case, the underlying issues were more important and the fact that she couldn't sleep at night was truly taking a toll on her health and her ability to concentrate.

I had mistakenly assumed that she wasn't sleeping because of work worries or some kind of stress but it turned out that her bedroom was the cause of her sleeplessness. She was simply dropping her clothes to the floor and walking over them to get on to a bed that was already covered in her work paraphernalia and a mix of dirty and newly washed clothes.

We discussed her bedroom in a way that most people think about their attic. But there was no getting out of it — she needed to de-clutter, to organise her wardrobes, to clean the room thoroughly so she could breathe properly in there and finally she needed to find a colour scheme that would soothe and calm her (as opposed to the bright red wall that faced her as she lay in bed).

The change in her was apparent for all to see. She became calmer and more focussed and you could sense the shift — the flow — in her. She had a new level of serenity to her.

It's amazing what a simple purple and gold scheme, with a clear floor and all her jewellery displayed beautifully can do for a girl.

Is your bedroom calming or stressful?

PART II
Dream space

Do you remember your dreams? And do they make sense to you? Do you write them down and analyse them or barely even share them with your partner?

I'm not talking about your nocturnal meanderings here, I'm talking about your other dreams – the dream of being a rock star, of moving to Italy to write a book, of retiring to the countryside, of taking your yachtsman qualifications, of losing that weight, of having an amazing party for a big anniversary, of taking up a new hobby, be it Tae Kwon Do or crocheting, of spending more time with your elderly parents, of planning more activities with your kids.

Where do you dream? Where do your thoughts take flight? Is it in bed on a Sunday morning as you lie with your partner without the worries of the workweek yet in your mind? Or do you lie in bed at night and fantasise about how you'd like your home to be, or what Christmas will be like this year with the kids at just the perfect Father Christmas age? Do you sneak off in the day time and lie on your bed with the sun streaming through the window on you as you contemplate your future – your plans to return to work or to set up a business of your own?

We all need somewhere to dream. There's no perfect place to dream other than the one that you think is right for you. However, once you know where that space is it's important to design and decorate it to inspire you, to make you feel like you can genuinely achieve those dreams.

But how do we go about achieving our dreams? So many of us have left them behind, in favour of looking after someone else. We think we're too old or that our skills aren't relevant anymore, or that we're just not capable. Spending so much time in the home looking after young children can be very detrimental to a woman's self-esteem. It is not an easy job to look after little ones. And while others may look over our shoulders and think 'it doesn't look too bad', they could well be right, if only it were for just that day. It's the repetition that's tough, the day-in-day-out nature of the household chores and the children's demands.

There's no office party for the mums in town. An occasional coffee morning or night out with the girls can be supportive and fun yet we need as many avenues as possible to keep ourselves believing in what we are capable of doing – which is so much more than sweeping up Rice Krispies and picking up strewn toys.

We need to find the space – the head space and the physical space - so that we can make our dreams come true.

"You are never too old to set another goal or dream a new dream ... "
C.S. Lewis

What do you dream of doing? Are you comfortable even thinking about your ability to have dreams? How do you feel about sharing those dreams? Some of us are happy to share our goals, yet there are many more who would rather have their teeth pulled. Which one are you?

It's time you knew that your dreams are just as possible as the next person's. You are no less capable than anyone else. If Richard Branson can dream about colonising Mars, you can dream about getting a job again. If Dubai can be transformed from being a desert into a vibrant city serving millions, then you can burn off a few pounds of weight. If a Paralympian can control a galloping horse then you can write a book.

You just need to know the formula - the formula of how to succeed at achieving your dreams.

Success formula

I'll get straight to the point, because this is useful. There is a formula to make our dreams come true. It sounds too good to be true, of course, and I barely believed it myself, but once it's been pointed out, you'll see it time and time again – in movies, in literature, and in life.

The success formula is a way of thinking that brings about riches to those who seek wealth, slim thighs to those who yearn for svelte-ness and a beautiful home for the design and aesthetically minded. It is a formula that can be found in many books (The Secret, Think and Grow Rich) and has been shared many times before in many different formats (though never a + b = c). However, as evident by the lack of success in many aspects of our lives, the formula might well be easy to comprehend yet, in practice, can be a bit of a 'slippery little sucker' (in the words of Julia Roberts in Pretty Woman).

I have taken the principles from the success formula and have adapted them slightly to fit into the home world, but they are easily transferred back to the world of finance or weight loss if those are other goals you are considering pursuing. (Most of us are.)

Dwell-Being's success formula - COACH A

There are six steps in the success formula and they follow the acronym "COACH A". To me, Coach A means first class. It means luxury, and I believe we all deserve luxury and to travel in first class through life. It's not just something for 'other people'. Adopting this as a mindset will help you succeed too. Expecting to be successful and believing you deserve it are all part of this process.

The formula begins with a vision, a dream. I call this a concept, because this is language that designers use to encapsulate ideas. The concept is the most important step in the process and therefore takes the most time to explain. (Bear with it, the steps afterwards become increasingly easy).

C = Concept

A concept is your vision, or your dream. It is about knowing what you want. It doesn't start out as a fully fleshed-out plan with bullet point actions and a to-do list as long as your arm, those come as the idea progresses and gains momentum. A concept is the beginning, it is the bouncing board that gets your creative juices flowing. It is the basis from which everything else will come and it is, therefore, incredibly important to know it well, to be passionate about it and to give it as much of your attention as possible.

How to create, love and develop a concept

Designers, for the most part have plenty of creative juice, but they still look out for the "ah-ha moment" for every project. The ah-ha moment is the basis of the idea. It is their initial concept. (And it's very rarely a muse arriving waving her fairy wand and sprinkling magic dust everywhere.)

So how do ah-ha moments come about? Sadly, there is no 0800 number for them I'm afraid, and even discussing them can feel a little bit 'out there' and esoteric. What we know for sure is that these moments of inspiration arrive when we least expect them, which means we often have to sit and wait patiently for them. We have to believe in them and know they will come. It's fair to say that ah-ha moments require faith.

And what is faith? Faith is certainty. It's belief. It's not fixed solid but has a kind of fluidity and flexibility inherent in it. Faith is a dance with a strong partner who you trust implicitly.

What do you have faith in? Can you describe it? Where do you feel it? What does it look like or sound like? I suspect it's slightly different for us all. However, while faith might not be terribly easy to nail down and describe, it is something we all need and it *is* relatively easy to acquire.

As we have recognised, faith is based on certainty and this comes from experience – you've done it before, so you'll do it again. You have faith that the sun will come up tomorrow morning, because it's happened every day of your life so far. You have faith that your kids will walk in on you and your partner at a most inopportune moment on a Sunday morning, because, again, it's happened before, and you have faith in it happening again.

A walk in the park

Ironically, however, while me must have faith in our ability to be creative and for the blessed ah-ha moments to arrive, they rarely come when you try *too* hard. Doggedly trying to find the right idea will not bring about the results you are seeking. Strangely, a walk in the park is more likely to fire off your creativity than sitting hunched over a blank page and pleading for an idea to come. A brisk stroll allows your brain the room to breathe and create thoughts. It's amazing what oxygen, movement or maybe even a spot of rain will do for your creativity.

Our creativity and the much sought after inspiration tends to come when we are feeling relaxed and not focussing on a 'problem'. Haven't you noticed that you get great ideas when you're in the shower, or driving long distances, or on holiday and not thinking about anything more than the sun on your back? When your brain is given a bit of a breather then it will provide. (We'll be discussing this breathing space more in the next chapter).

Take, for example, when you've been asked a direct and rather tricky question, perhaps in front of a few people you feel judge you. With people watching over you, scrutinising you, you're not likely to come up with the best response. The perfect answer, be it witty, intelligent, biting or simply charming, won't come until you are driving home, or when you're telling a friend later. 'Oh I should have said that... I could kick myself.'

It's the same with your creativity. It doesn't like to feel judged, as if people are expecting it to 'perform'. Unless you have trained it otherwise (you're an improv actor or stand-up comedian, for example) then our creative brain far prefers to be left alone for a while. It likes to be given some room to ponder the parameters and nosey around some options for a while before coming up with the goods.

So how do you give your brain these 'parameters'?

Coincidence?

In Me Space you put together a concept board of the style you would like in your house. Have you noticed how your brain has started to spot items that match your new style? You might have been shopping and noticed the colour turquoise (or your chosen favourite colour) is suddenly everywhere, or the curved French style armoires you tore out of a magazine made an unexpected appearance in your email inbox, or the glassware you thought was 'just your style' featured on a TV programme. It's quite remarkable to see how these 'coincidences' start to appear. (Just like the hordes of pregnant women who seem to appear from nowhere as soon as you declare your own happy news).

But they're not coincidences. They're just your brain doing as you've asked it to do. In being very specific and spending some real time figuring out your own style, what you like and what you dislike, you are telling your brain what to pay attention to – you are giving it parameters. Some call this the law of attraction but I'll stick with the world of interiors, so in designer language, you have 'briefed' your brain to find those styles. And while it feels quite extraordinary for them to 'suddenly' start appearing in your life, the truth is that they were there all along, it's just that your brain is now wired to pick up the message. (To be accurate it was the reticular activating system (RAS) in your brain. Good to know, huh?)

What do you focus on?

What is it that you want your brain to pay attention to?
Your brain only reports back what you have briefed it to
look out for. So if you're thinking and saying to yourself
that there's no point in trying to make any changes (to
your home, to your life, to your body, or to your
relationships) then your brain will go and search for
evidence of that. If you tell your brain repeatedly to focus
on the horrific lives of some of the soap opera characters,
then it will honestly believe the world is a miserable
place. If you focus on the news, then again you will learn
to believe that the world is dangerous and unpredictable.
If, on the other hand, you pay attention to the more
positive aspects of your life, your brain will go in a new
direction in search of evidence to prove you are right. If
you focus on how helpful and considerate your son is,
then you will, all of a sudden, start to find examples and
stories of him being this way.

Using this principle to good effect is how to harness your
dreams. If you focus (and by this I mean spend time
with, talk about, look for pictures that resemble exactly
what you're thinking about) on your dreams and goals
then your brain will go to the trouble of finding ways for
you to achieve those goals.

This is not difficult to understand, it is almost common
sense, it does, however, require faith. You have to have
faith in your goals and dreams and more importantly
you have to have faith in the idea that your brain will
work *with* you to achieve them. All you have to do is
'brief' it correctly.

Briefing your brain

Before a designer expects anything of their creative mind, they think through some basic 'parameters' and considerations.

- Why is the project being undertaken?
    - A need for more space.
    - A revamp.
    - A change in lifestyle.
    - A new home.
- Who are the people who live here? What are they really like?
    - Travel frequently.
    - Watch the telly a lot.
    - Have parties.
    - Exercise at home.
    - Have a passion for drumming.
- What already exists in the property (if anything exists yet)?
    - Lovely parquet floor.
    - Window overlooking the bins.
    - Neighbours with noisy habits.
    - An acre site in woodland.

Designers establish the fundamentals of the project and these help to shape ideas, moving them in certain directions (keeping the parquet floor) and refusing to let them go in others (don't highlight the window with the view of the bins). These considerations provide the outline of the project and help the designer to foresee how the room, or the home, will look and feel.

Once they have gained this understanding, however, they won't just rush ahead into creating a quick-fix solution. The solution will evolve over time. Ideas, ah-ha moments, will come with ease once the parameters have been clearly understood. Set the brain off in the right direction but then give it a breather (perhaps a walk, as recommended by the author Stephen King, or a period of rest, as was apparently Einstein's habit) and then have faith that it will come back with some wonderful answers and a creative solution.

Having a concept gives us direction. It helps us focus the mind on what we want to achieve. At this stage we don't need all the specifics, they will come over time, as we discuss the idea, nurture it and let it grow, but to begin with we need the germ of a concept. A vision. A dream. Love your dreams!

O = Oomph

Tenacity, dogged determination and blinkered focus, or what I call 'oomph' (it's the Yorkshire in me...) are key elements in the success formula. They are an easy explanation of why people do not succeed (because without these, we simply give up.)

- It's too difficult.
- It's not right for me.
- Someone told me I was doing the wrong thing.
- It didn't succeed the first time, so it must be a duff idea.

These are the reasons (or excuses) why people fail. And while it's easy to read them and think, 'I'd never do that', the truth is, there are quitters all around us. We look at the odds, we look at our previous results, we measure how far out of our comfort zone we'll need to go in order to make things happen and we turn to the TV and the sofa, or the pub, when we realise it's going to be hard work.

On the other hand, there are the examples of those who ploughed through the doubts, who ignored the negative (and rather annoying) voices in their heads and who knuckled down to make sure they achieved their dreams. These are the athletes who got up at 5am, without fail, to practice their sport, they are the inventors and scientists who started again time and time again, thinking not 'we have failed' but 'we have found a way not to achieve our goal, now we must continue until we find a way *to* achieve our goal.' They are the bands who practised and played wherever they could find the opportunity, and the comedians who trawled the circuit committed to making people laugh and determined to be spotted by the right person in the crowd.

Instant gratification

We have our brains filled with ideas that success is easy, because we watch TV shows that instantly glorify young talent, where secret agents are recruited from the street, where models are spotted while out shopping and where unique thoughts just pop into people's heads. And while there are examples of these miracles happening, no doubt, the statistics would suggest that this route is not worth relying on. The hard work and determination route is a far safer path. Anyone who you consider a success (in whatever aspect of their life) will tell you so. The stockbroker can explain the long, stressful hours involved, the footballer can walk you through the training they put in day-in day-out and the bikini model can take you to the gym and show you her workout and the truth about how little she eats. To know what is required and to still continue requires grit, commitment and oomph.

And while you might think that this seems a little dramatic when it comes to re-designing your home, you might possibly think again when you're half way through your refurbishment (certainly if you're doing major structural work). Stress levels go up when your life is full of dust. You need to be committed to see it through.

A = Advice and accountability

On the whole, people do not wake up one day, concept in mind, determination in pocket and think 'I have everything I need to achieve my goal'. Certainly not if it's a goal they haven't achieved before. For the most part, they need to get some advice on how to move forward.

Information is a valuable thing and fortunately we live in a day and age where it is available with great ease. In fact, we have so much information available that it can often become overwhelming. Today it isn't a case of looking for help, it's more a case of finding the person we can trust (or simply like) to provide the information for us.

We trust people we know and like - people who are just like us. It's a human thing (or perhaps a bird thing) because we tend to flock together. We take advice from other people who have been in situations similar to ourselves and have achieved the results we are also looking to achieve. Don't we?

As we move along with this project you will need to seek advice from a variety of people. I am here to set you off, to help with your concept and to give you some structure to follow, but as I don't know the specifics of your home, or what you want to achieve, I can't help you fine-tune the design or even assist with the gorgeous-but-tricky-to-put-up wallpaper. You will need advice on the simple (paint finishes, carpet types) and also the more complicated (electrical circuitry, kitchen design).

Dwell-Being tip

It's a good idea to get a little black book (or iPhone) of advisors. Feel good about having a suite of tradesmen at your disposal. (Collect them as you would do shoes.) Have one who is an expert in plumbing and another who can explain the joys of joinery. Appreciate them for their skills and the information they have accrued from years of being a plumber or a joiner. If you treat them well, and respect their profession, they will do likewise. As long as you're giving them clear instructions – wishy-washy doesn't cut it with most tradesmen.

So, isn't it a good job you've spent that time really discovering what it is you want to achieve? Doesn't it feel good to know that you have a clear vision of what you want to get done, a determination to do it and reassurance that there are thousands of people out there who will be happy to advise you?

Modelling

It's worth noting that advisors don't necessarily need to be someone with whom we have actual contact. They don't need to be someone we can call up on the phone. They can simply be role models, someone who is a great example of what we are setting out to achieve. If we 'model' the 'roles' of that person, we are likely to also enjoy the results that they have achieved.

Modelling success is simply watching very carefully how someone who is accomplished in the field is already doing it. It's important to understand how they think, how they behave, how they communicate, even their body language. Think of this in the same way a dragon from the den would assess a business model, in order to understand the structure of the organisation, its operational hierarchy and its product suite. If we look at the strategies and structure of a successful person and break down their habits, we can really understand what makes them successful. And if we then replicate these habits and strategies accurately, we are more likely to follow in their path.

If I'm honest, when I first heard the theory of 'modelling', I thought it sounded a little like cheating, almost

Niki Schäfer

plagiarism. How could I just copy someone else? It seemed fake and lacked integrity at best, and felt almost 'Single, White, Female' (remember that movie?) at worst. So I started to use the word 'strategy' instead, following a 'strategy' wasn't cheating. It was sensible.

'Strategy' to me (and I stress this being personal because as I've discussed in previous chapters, words matter. 'Strategy' works for me, but it might not for you. That being said, 'modelling' might not have been an issue for you in the first place! I digress...) strategy is a concept, broken down into a practical application. A strategy is a pattern of how we behave and, as an interior designer, I understand the concept of patterns. Patterns aren't only pretty pictorial flowers on wallpaper they are also blueprints or architectural drawings and accurate drawings are a fundamental part of the design process. They need to be easy to read. This idea was starting to work in my world. I can read a blueprint. So I can follow a strategy. As a result, I can model someone else's behaviour. And so can you.

Strategies

How do you find great strategies?

- Read autobiographies, they reveal so much about how successful celebrities and talented individuals think and react to circumstances.
- Use online resources, which are full of success strategy information. There's a plethora of blogs on how to be successful and You Tube videos on every subject imaginable. It's almost difficult to

avoid! Try www.TED.com for some truly inspiring, short talks in the technology, entertainment and design arenas.

- Read magazines and papers that focus on solid content rather than a cheap, gossip-based slant.
- Look around your everyday life for good role models. They already exist in every aspect of your life.

Everyday examples

If I'm stressed about something that's going on with the kids, I'll look around to see who can help me. I won't choose another stress-head to talk to; I'll find someone who seems to have the situation under control. I might not walk up and say 'How on earth do you get your kids to behave?' but I might watch how they treat them, the words they use, their patience levels and their kindness. And I'll go about adopting these 'strategies'. They've worked for someone else, there's no reason why they won't work for me.

When it comes to a successful home, find people whose home strategies you admire. Are there any people who you'd like to model? Someone who adores baking and their kitchen is always a flurry of activity. Is that something you'd like to introduce into your home? Then go and hang out with that woman and 'model' her. If you want to be more organised and efficient and you have a friend who is never late and whose children never forget their homework, then go and see how things are run in her home. Model her behaviour. I'm sure you can think of many other examples.

Taking advice doesn't need to mean sitting attentively listening to someone else lecturing you. It can be a quiet investigation or it can be a friendly interview. As long as you understand that advice is paramount. Because going it alone can be lonely and unnecessarily difficult.

A = Accountability

A also stands for accountability, another fundamental part of the success formula. Sharing your dreams with others and committing to making them happen can have a considerable impact on your motivation and your focus. Knowing you are seeing someone next week who is likely to check up on your progress might be just the kick up the derriere you sorely need. They needn't be mean, or sergeant major like, they might simply ask 'What's been happening?' but having them there will do a lot for your progress, I can assure you.

This method is used on all kinds of weight loss programmes, for example, and is the key principle behind coaching. The idea is simply to have someone who will check in with you on a regular basis to make sure that you are doing the things that *you've* said *you* want to do. There's no judgement involved, it's your dreams they're asking about, not their own.

Find someone to share your concept with and give them some key dates by which you'd like to have achieved things ('I want to have found an architect by spring', 'I'll have spoken to the plumber by the end of the week', 'I'll have shown my husband the expensive cabinets I like over the weekend...'). Become accountable. Stick to the promises you've made yourself. If you become accountable, you're almost guaranteed success, (especially if you follow the other rules too.)

C = Confidence

Having faith in ourselves is something we all need and self-belief is another important aspect of the success formula. When you listen to someone speaking confidently, don't you believe her or him? Don't you know that somehow their dreams will come true? Confidence has a way of drawing us in, we pay attention to it, and we yearn to feel like it.

Confidence is definitely required when it comes to designing your home and as an interior designer, I spend a lot of time dealing with confidence. For the most part, people fear change and yet they desperately want things to be better. I give people the confidence to go ahead. This book has been written so that *you* can feel the confidence to create the home *you* really want.

Confidence is about knowing what you want. It's being so sure about it that you can ask (or tell) other people what to do in order to get it done. If someone is lacking confidence, on the other hand, it's because they're not sure of what they want. More importantly, they're not sure of *why* they want it. It is fundamental to understand why you want to do something, why you want something a certain way. This gives you certainty and with certainty comes confidence – even in the face of a decorator sucking his teeth and saying 'Sorry love, I've been in this business for 15 years and I've never seen it done like that. Are you sure?' Say 'Yes I am sure'. (Because yes, you are sure.)

I get great delight in hearing trades people coming to me at the end of the job and saying 'I was a bit worried about your choices there Niki, but I've got to hand it to you, it looks right super!'

This level of confidence comes from me investigating what is important to my clients about their home, what their tastes are, why they live the way they live, what order they work in, what inspires them, what they enjoy, how they relax, how they approach life. I dig down so that I can provide answers that are designed just for them. I am confident about what they truly want. And once I'm confident, *then* I apply the interior design tools. What I call the 'how-to'.

H = How-to

Here's a home truth: there is simply no way that you, or I, can know it all. The impact of every stain on every wood, the engineering involved in a cantilever staircase, the precision and craftsmanship to make a drawer that looks stunning and closes with a whoosh and a gentle click? I might know a little about all these topics but I need an expert who will actually do the job. And you do too. There's no better advice than to surround yourself by people who know more than you do and having a great design team is very reassuring. Expecting yourself to do it all is brutal, so learn the core skills that suit your way of thinking and delegate everything else.

Basic skills

- Can you make curtains? Maybe yes, maybe no.
- Can you measure the window? Of course you can.
- Can you paint the walls? Maybe yes, maybe no.
- Can you choose the paint colour? Of course you can.
- Can you design a bathroom? Maybe yes, maybe no.
- Can you pick the bath mat and matching towels? Of course you can.
- Can you lay the flooring? Maybe yes, maybe no.
- Can you pick out a rug? Of course you can.

Designer skill set

What are the skills you need to design a home? (Out of interest, these are not the same skills as being an interior designer. Being an interior designer is about running a business, and designing is, in truth, a very small percentage of the work involved.)

Do you have these skills? (I know you do...)

Skill 1 – Understanding the bigger picture.

For what purpose are you designing your home? Do you need to convert the attic because your son needs some privacy and an escape from his three sisters? Or are you re-organising and sprucing up the utility room because you're bored senseless of the dog sleeping in the clean clothes?

You learnt these skills in Head Space. You understand your 'why?' behind everything you want to do now.

Skill 2 – Looking objectively

What does the building or the room have to offer? What are the design considerations? This requires a clear mind to look objectively at the situation and assess what is already working and what needs to be changed.

You learnt these skills in Outer Space. You understand the meaning of home and what to take into consideration.

Skill 3 – Understanding, appreciating and negotiating taste and style

What do you like? What do you dislike? It's extremely important to have a clear idea of what you think looks good and what doesn't. Equally you need to appreciate the taste of other people. Being open-minded will make life easier, however, compromise will only lead to unhappiness (probably in both parties). A solution has to be designed. There is always a win-win solution. Always.

You learnt these skills in Me Space and in Thinking Space. You can find the ideas that will make everyone happy.

Skill 4 – Communicating with patience and clarity

Communication is the number one skill of an interior designer.

- We must listen impeccably (and then replay what we have heard, so that no wires are crossed).
- We must talk about colour and shapes that exist in people's heads (how vague is that?) and must then get them safe and sound into someone else's head (alas mind reading is not on the curriculum).
- We must deliver good news, ('The auction was a huge success and the rare Chinese chest is yours!') but frequently also have to deliver bad news. ('Sorry, your walls are completely rotten and must be replaced immediately, wiping out 10% of your budget...').
- We must explain why things cost so much money, how much time things take and why deliverymen are the way deliverymen are.
- We must take an idea and translate it into a reality for our clients while their lives are turned upside down, the children are covered in dust and no one can find anything in the kitchen for six months.
- Communication is key.

You learnt these skills in Thinking Space. And while you may not have clients to involve, you will undoubtedly have a partner to explain your choices to, parents-in-law who come and visit and ask why you chose that particular combi-boiler and a variety of tradesmen who you will want to keep briefed, updated and on schedule. All of this requires the patience of a new parent and the communication skills of a legal mediator. Alternatively, you can shout a lot. But be prepared for the stresses and strains to show in a variety of other areas of your life (your relationships, your health, your bank balance).

Skill 5 – Practical skills

From measuring a room and drawing it up accurately, to taking down fabric codes and understanding fire regulations, there are a number of very practical skills involved in interior design. Having the ability to switch from an artistic head space into a practical consideration head space is very important.

You learnt these skills in Head Space and in Dream Space.

Skills 6 – Completion

It can be very easy to start a decorating project, or something of an even larger nature, and then be dragged down by it. I have seen many bathrooms that aren't quite finished and homes that have squares of experimental paint in patches around the house (and have been that way for years). 'Cracking on' until the job is done requires determination and grit. And that starts with a commitment at the beginning of the project to do 'whatever it takes' and perseverance to see you through 'whatever comes your way'.

You are committing to seeing this project through, with every page you read of this book. Congratulations!

Acquiring these skills (or delegating the tasks to others) will make your design project run smoothly and efficiently and that is all part of a calm, sane home. Enjoying the process of creating it is almost as important as living happily in it afterwards!

A = Action

Jim Rohn's definition of failure:
'A few errors in judgement repeated every day.'

Jim Rohn's definition of success:
'A few simple disciplines practised every day.'

After all this thinking, all this believing and all this faith, comes doing. We have to actually do something (if a change in the right direction is going to be achieved. I say 'in the right direction' purposefully because things will change around you even if you don't act. There is no such thing as staying still. There are always consequences.)

In the first chapter I asked whether you'd ever watched interior design shows on TV, and then been disappointed to find that nothing has changed in your own home. We've all been taken on a fabulous journey with the home owners who were building their dream home and in our minds, we too worked long into the cold nights and spent hours assessing roof tile suitability. But then the programme ends and reality hits. Our home hasn't changed. (Because we did nothing... obviously!)

However, action does not mean that you have to launch yourself from the sofa to knocking down a wall. Action needn't be a huge step, and certainly nothing as decisive as removing a wall. It can be small, and in fact, it's often better that way.

Small actions build momentum

These simple acts cost nothing but have huge impact as they set you off on the right trajectory. They are the beginning of your journey.

- Pick up the phone and discuss your idea with someone you trust. Once the idea is out, once it has been shared, it will be bounced back to you in a different format and from a different perspective. As a result, it will have grown. Someone will have added another dimension to your initial thought.
- Send an email out and ask someone to come and have a look at the sticking sliding doors you've dreamt of turning into beautiful bi-folds.
- Knock on a neighbour's door and ask about the builder they used last year.
- Call the hotel you stayed in at Easter and ask them where they got the bedroom carpet you so loved.
- Go through all the magazines you already own and pull together your concept board!

Every action will build upon the next. Celebrate as you move along and feel the momentum building. Take one step at a time, keep your eyes on the goal and know where you're heading but don't feel you have to get there in one fell swoop. There's no need to feel overwhelmed. Just break it down into small manageable-sized chunks and do one thing at a time. Before you know it huge progress will have been made and soon after that your project will be complete. You'll then be ready to move on to the next room!

Dwell-Being success formula summary

COACH A is an easy acronym to remember that will keep you on track – concept, oomph, advice & accountability, confidence, how-to and, most importantly, action.

Homework

Look at the formula again and assess yourself against it. Look at your past projects, recognising which ones were incredibly successful (arranging a family holiday, planning your wedding, finding your first job) and see how this formula relates to what happened. Equally, look at the projects that haven't quite got off the ground or those that haven't been finished, which element of the formula was missing?

Is this a pattern? Is the 'missing element' something you miss out time and time again?

- Are your ideas a bit vague?
- Do you quit too soon?
- Do you always think you can do it all by yourself?
- Do you lose confidence half way through?
- Do you simply not have the right skills?
- Do you dream a lot but, in reality, do diddly squat about making it happen?

Be honest. Be aware of these things and remember them for next time. Anticipate what's ahead and be prepared. This is the way to make it work. This project is going to work. Your home will be outrageously gorgeous and a calm, sane space for you and your family.

Summary

You have learned how to measure a room accurately and produce a plan so that you can share your ideas with others. We have used the bedroom as a basic room layout but the principles are exactly the same for all rooms, so you have the ability to do this for the whole house now.

We have also looked at your ability to dream and what it takes to make those dreams come true.

Homework

- Measure a room and create a plan (scale 1:50) showing the layout of the furniture.
- Assess your past projects against the COACH A formula. Recognise where you have succeeded in the past. Celebrate your achievement!
- Consider where you have previously failed and make suitable plans so that it won't happen for this project. Tell someone about this (be accountable).

Congratulations

You have learnt an invaluable skill that will be useful for every room and space you ever live and work in. This ability to be able to put ideas on to paper where they are easily 'played with' makes life so much easier and will mean you'll never have to return a sofa that's too big or a cabinet that didn't fit ever again!

You've also examined the skill sets that make you successful. If you're a fabulous gardener, you'll be using all the steps in the success formula, if you're a magnificent meringue baker, it's because you use the formula. Except you probably don't know it. Until now, you've simply done well the things you do well. And you've become frustrated at what hasn't worked for you. Now you have the tools to understand what works. Now you have the skills to make the necessary changes. Or delegate them to someone else (did I mention that already? Some things are worth hammering home you know!).

In the next chapter we'll be having a bit of a breather. You can put your feet up. What is more, you can tell everyone around you it's homework.

FOUNDATION 2: FAMILY THINKING

Space 6 - Breathing Space

"You cannot find yourself by going into the past. You can find yourself by coming into the present."
Eckhart Tolle

DWELL-BEING MODEL

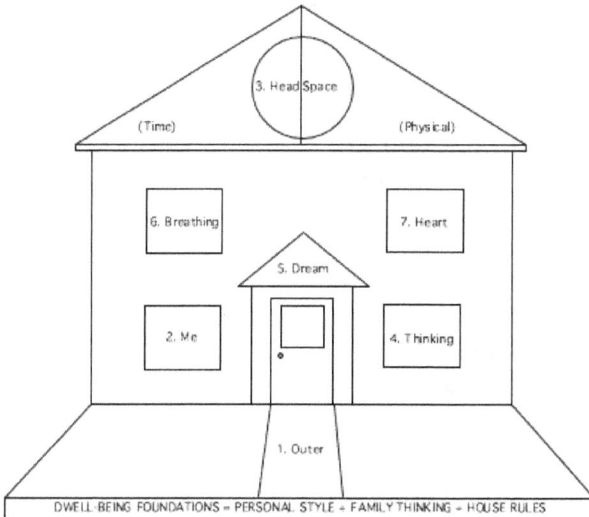

3. Head Space

(Time)   (Physical)

6. Breathing   7. Heart

5. Dream

2. Me   4. Thinking

1. Outer

DWELL-BEING FOUNDATIONS = PERSONAL STYLE + FAMILY THINKING + HOUSE RULES

Outer Space
o The concept of home is something you are willing to share and discuss with others.
o You are really proud of the approach to your home. It makes you smile as you walk up to your door. You actually feel sanity return as you walk into your home.

Me Space
o You can walk into a shop and dismiss 75% of the items in there immediately. They're not your style. What a time saver.

Head Space
o Your home within your home is now fully established.
o Your time-management skills are becoming noticeable to you (and others).

Thinking Space
o You've started to change the way you talk to your husband, using the words associated with his thinking style and are amazed at the positive results it has brought about.

Dream Space
o You have measured up your bedroom and played with a few layouts. You know exactly what the room needs (and have written a 'to buy' list).
o You've spent a little time pondering your successes and your failures. You feel a curious sense of confidence in your future projects.

Breathing Space
o You're now going to learn how to craft places to relax.
o And establish space to connect with family and friends and to just 'be'.

Heart Space
o   How to organise places to eat and be together.
o   And build space to feel, to listen, to be heard and to be loved.

Conclusion
o   House rules - dos and don'ts.
o   A celebration of huge proportions.

Breathing space chapter outcome

By the end of this chapter you will:

- Have recalibrated yourself back in to being a human being (rather than a human doing).
- Have learnt how to design a relaxing environment.
- Understand how to create a decorative scheme from your image selection.
- Know the joy of being grateful - for the silliest and the most magnificent of everything.
- Have noticed a distinct lack of witty asides (my charming little observations in brackets) in this chapter. This is what happens when you get into the nitty-gritty of the matter. I can't laugh this stuff off. This is seriously how to be calm, sane and happy.

Home truth

'I can't hear myself think,' we say. No one pays any attention. The TV continues to blare, the iPad adds another conversation from a different TV show and the DS game bleeps and squeals from the other side of the room. We look at the children and wonder how they can even focus on their games, or their TV, while there is so much 'interference' in the air. We consider sending them all to their rooms so we can have a quiet moment to ourselves but fear that it will be the start of a slippery slope and our children will disappear from our lives altogether, their bedrooms becoming a refuge from where they communicate only via avatars in a graphically designed world.

Today we are spending more and more time at our screens. We communicate via texts and tweets and Facebook and hold our friendship statistics as a proud tally at the top of our home pages. We find it amusing the first time we send a text to someone in the house, in the next room, the hilarity of it but then it turns into a habit. 'Tea time, come downstairs.'

Oxytocin

Our biology requires that we look at each other. Looking into someone's eyes as we communicate releases oxytocin (the feel good chemical you'll have read and heard much about when you were pregnant or breast feeding). However, we are slowly moving away from being able to access this chemical (also called the love or cuddle hormone) due to the way we are behaving. Today, we barely make eye contact with others at all. Admittedly, prolonged eye contact can be awkward (especially if it's with the wrong person, or they have food remains on their face) but today we are almost avoiding any eye contact at all. We feel much safer behind a screen. We're also far less likely to pick up the phone and speak to someone these days, thinking a text message is as good as a call. (I don't envy the kids of today, getting dumped by text must be worse than your best friends passing the message on to you).

What impact is this having on our relationships? I wonder. Equally, what impact is this having on us, on our own happiness and our own well-being? When we have so many choices of technology to entertain ourselves with, do we neglect our own need for a bit of peace and quiet? Don't we revert to a quick look on Facebook rather than spending the time to have a quiet moment to ourselves? It's worth considering, are you addicted to social media, or texting, and what impact is this having on you and those around you?

(Did you just skip over that last question? Really, it's a biggy...so please give it the same consideration you'd give an urgent beep on your phone.)

The power of peace and quiet

While those with small children yearn for the sound of silence, in the same way a winning team is desperate to hear the final whistle blow, we don't always appreciate that silence when we get it. We rush around in it, emptying dishwashers or taking the bins out or tidying up. The idea of just sitting and breathing and enjoying the peace and quiet seems indulgent and frivolous (or maybe just a bit middle aged, so we pick up a magazine in case anyone should walk in and catch us just staring into space.) But there is genuine power in peace and quiet. It isn't just something you can hear the voices of your own parents begging for. It's a necessity.

A personal note

I've never been one to sit down and I was proud of how full my days were. 'I haven't sat down all day' would have a ring of pride in its statement. I'd fill my brain (more input, more input) and talk non-stop (more output, more output) and in the minutes in between I'd just 'do'. I couldn't stop. What is more, the idea of stopping almost frightened me. If there was nothing for me to do then what did that mean about me? It meant something was missing, or more to the point, I felt I was missing out on something somebody else was doing. I do not like to be left out.

The idea of stopping and letting my brain empty itself, quieten down, and have a breather, sounded like torture to me. I imagined monks sitting high in the Himalayas quietly meditating, contemplating the universe. This was not a comforting thought. It was downright uncomfortable, in fact.

Slowing down lessons

I learnt the skills of time management (as I shared with you in Head Space) and the ability to 'max out' my days with all the things I wanted to accomplish. This was motivating to me. This was the direction I wanted to be heading in. Until soon, perhaps a year after living this way, I discovered that the endless energy I had to begin with was starting to falter. My response? To go to the gym more. I needed to build stronger muscles, push myself harder, and work my way through it. And yet, weeks later, I simply felt depleted.

My mum told me to slow down. And I'm afraid I must admit that I did not pay a single iota of attention to her. (Sorry, Mum). I pushed on. And then one day, whilst 'gently' boxing in the gym, without gloves (clearly a foolish decision but at the time I was simply following instructions), I sprained my thumb.

Now, while a sprained thumb might not be the most serious injury in the world, it is incredibly debilitating (especially as I was given the chunkiest brace on the planet to protect it). The gym was a complete no-go (just the impact of movement made the thumb ache), computer work was out, writing by hand was not a possibility, driving was uncomfortable and reading was clunky. I was left to sit and do nothing. I literally had nothing else I could do but relax.

I was sad about this at first. It seemed such a waste of my precious time but soon, I became aware of a rather pleasant ember inside me. It was unfamiliar but welcoming, it was slow and steady rather than the usual galloping sensations I associate with feeling good. I let it build (to be honest, I had little choice) and I acclimatized to the feeling. It felt a little like being on holiday (but without the bikini). It felt like a lazy lunch with friends (but without the white wine), it felt almost like those first days of bringing a new born baby home when the world stops and the idea of anyone working and living 'normal life' seems impossible. I started to savour the sensation.

Pause

Sitting in a theatre before an orchestra starts, we hear the warm-up as instruments are fine-tuned, and musicians settle into place. The sounds are not unpleasant but they are chaotic – they are the sounds of a number of individuals doing their own thing. As the conductor enters, a hush descends. He taps his baton loudly, several taps, and all eyes are on him. The musicians, instruments in place, gather their thoughts. Pause. Pause. And then they play in unison.

It is the pause that has united them.

This moment of pause is something we could all do with in our daily life. It is this moment of consideration, this focus on what needs to be achieved, on who we are speaking to (or playing with), that enables us to move ahead seamlessly. It is this moment that will stop us simply reacting out of habit, or presuming that we know what to do, without even listening. It is only a moment, but its results are powerful because this moment of pause has captured our attention. And our attention has the magic and power of the universe in it (which obviously sounds completely melodramatic but which has in fact been proven in quantum physics. And, while here might not be the place to go into the finer details, it's worth noting that it's true.) Your attention is your life. As we have discussed in previous chapters, what you focus on, is the meaning you have given to your own life. It's you who chooses to focus on it. It's you who gives it meaning. So choose wisely where you put your attention.

A pause is a moment of assessment. It is preparation. It is focus. Sadly however, we tend to see this type of thinking as only necessary for work, large projects or when the children seriously need organising. The truth, however, is that we need to do this for ourselves. Frequently. We need to stop and smell the roses every now and again. We need to be grateful for what we've got. And let me be bold enough to say that this isn't a Sunday school lesson. Gratitude is a skill we have skipped over for the past couple of generations (probably in favour of some technological feel good factor of getting on to the next level in the computer game instead). And it has been to our detriment.

"When a person doesn't have gratitude, something is missing in his or her humanity."
Elie Wiesel

Time to appreciate

After a hard day of work, isn't it nice to come into a home where you feel you can breathe freely, where you can let go of all the day's hassles and simply relax? After a Sunday dinner, when everything has been put away and the dishwasher is whirring, isn't it great to sit and appreciate what's gone on, the hard work that was put into cooking the food, the conversation and family nonsense that went on at the meal? Isn't it an amazing sensation to observe the chaos after the frenzy of present opening on Christmas morning? Isn't that quiet moment the one you can still see in your mind's eye? Why are we always rushing on to the next thing when there's so much to reflect on right now?

Do you take the time to look over your day, your week or your month and think about what you've done, what's worked for you, and what hasn't? Or do you constantly live in the future, always planning ahead or 'working out what could go wrong'? Taking the time to look backwards instead of forwards all the time, to re-live the good moments and to gain an understanding of the not-so-good moments is fundamental. How else can we learn? How else do we know what to amend? How else do we really know what we loved to do? How else do we express gratitude?

Attitude of gratitude

Tony Robbins, a peak performance coach and an extraordinary speaker, talks about an 'attitude of gratitude'. And while the rhyming might be for the benefit of an American audience (of course we Brits don't need such things, do we? We'd adopt an attitude of thankfulness, just to be awkward) it does stick in your head – especially if you apply an American accent when you say it. An additood of graditood.

"Living in this emotional state will enhance your life more than almost anything I know of. Cultivating this is cultivating life. Live with an attitude of gratitude."
Tony Robbins

Learning to be grateful is a skill much like any other. And it is a skill that will most certainly contribute to the happiness of your house. It might not be as obvious as measuring skills or learning how to coordinate colours but it is a thinking skill and a part of the science of a calm, sane home. Let me explain.

The science of gratitude

Our bodies are made up of cells. We are simply a mass of cells and if you looked under a microscope you'd see that these cells vibrate. If you sit quietly, I'm sure you can feel that sense of vibration in your body, the tingling in your ears as the blood moves through them, and the pounding of your heart. When you stand next to a loud speaker can't you feel your whole body reverberate? The sound has made your cells vibrate strongly.

Something else to make your cells vibrate strongly is emotion. When you're feeling romantic and gazing over the dinner table at your loved one, can't you feel your heart vibrating? When you watch your children on stage, singing their little hearts out, don't you feel almost 'fit to burst'? When you're angry, don't you physically shake? And when you're peaceful don't you feel the sensation of calm wash over you? Every emotion has a certain vibration. Every person has his or her own vibration (their norm) and then varying other vibrations depending on their mood.

As I've mentioned before, we humans like to stick together, we are attracted to people who are similar to us. On a physical level, we are attracted to someone who literally vibrates at the same frequency as us. That's why we 'resonate' with people. We're little 'similarity seeking beacons'. We search for more of what we've got. This means that if you're vibrating at an angry frequency you're more likely to seek out other people who have anger in their system. If you're at peace and float through life, you're more likely to surround yourself by people who are equally blissed out. And if you're grateful, you are more likely to encounter other people who are also grateful. What is more, you are more likely to encounter more gratitude because you have programmed your body and your mind to seek out more of this feel good factor. By practising gratitude you will find more things to be grateful about. It's the opposite of one of those vicious circles that seem so popular. Instead you can create a virtuous circle.

Question: And how on earth do I do that?
Answer: By making gratitude a habit.

Good habits

You need to get into the habit of being thankful. More importantly you need to *feel* grateful, not just a throw away thanks, but to feel it sincerely. You have to literally vibrate at the frequency of gratitude. That's what's going to be the attracting force. That's what's going to resonate with other things and people that are of the same frequency.

"Be grateful, honour the ordinary."
Brene Brown

I write a gratitude diary every night. I write five (new) things each night that I'm grateful for. I started to do this because some kooky guy who seemed happy suggested it was a good idea. I was a little cynical but more importantly I was curious and I was willing to give it a go. I've been doing it now for years and the transformation in my life is undeniable.

Before
- Mood swings – very high highs but lows that could last for days.
- Very short on patience.
- A façade of confidence.

After
- An almost constant sensation of contentedness, happiness or bliss.
- Considerably more patient (but still no angel, I'm afraid).
- A genuine confidence.

This is homework that I'd like you to do every day for the rest of your life, what is more I'd like you to encourage your children to do likewise (so it becomes a habit for them and they don't have to learn to do this, the way you are having to learn). On one hand, it's hard-core, yet on the other, it's incredibly simple. But don't let its simplicity fool you into thinking it's not necessary. This is one of the keys to your life.
- Air
- Water
- Food
- Gratitude

Get your priorities straight and make it a habit. It is habits like these that will guarantee you the calm and happy home you're looking for.

Homework

Write a gratitude diary every night for the rest of your life.

Start by being grateful for the big things, your marriage, your children, the fact that you have a roof over your head and live in a country at peace. Then begin to look into your every day, write down quotes from your kids (the things you've always said you'll write down, but always forget to do). Note what lessons you've learnt (the good and the bad). Be thankful for the strategies you've developed to cope with irritating teachers or whingeing children, be grateful for the check-out girl at your supermarket, or a taxi ride, or your mum's Yorkshire puddings. At the end of each day, lie in bed and think back over your day and write down the best part of it. And on the days when things haven't been all rosy, then be grateful for your ability to apologise perhaps, or your patience (even if it was only miniscule). Focus on the aspects of your life that you want to be grateful for. And if your day's been really that bad, then be grateful for something huge again – the Internet perhaps, or the street lamps that work, or the sun rising without fail.

It is well documented that soon you will have no difficulty whatsoever thinking of things to be grateful for, in fact during the day you'll start to look out for stuff. Nice flowers, a great cuppa, an unexpected email from an old friend, a funny comedian, a killer workout at the gym. Soon you'll be tuned into the idea of being grateful and without knowing it and you'll have become so much happier as a result. Because happiness comes when you're thankful for everything that's going on in your life.

Where to be grateful

I take the opportunity to write my gratitude diary lying in bed at the end of the day but throughout the day, I'm also now in the habit of sitting and breathing for a while and just soaking up what's good. I particularly love to do this on trains (the sensation of movement must vibrate me into gratitude) but I also love to do this at home. I have a chair where I can put my legs up and soak up what's going on around me. It's an area of pause and contemplation and happiness. It's an area I'd encourage you to find in your own home.

It doesn't matter where it is. It doesn't have to be a haven or a meditation room full of Buddha heads and incense burning, it's just somewhere you can stop every now and again and breathe. Make it a comfy chair, with a great view, somewhere you can sit with a cup of tea and just ponder. Don't let the fear that others might catch you with your feet up put you off. You are not being lazy or wasting time! You are breathing. You are being grateful. Tell them (the voices in your head, that is) that it's soul work.

There's no need to make an elaborate meditation zone with periods of silence that the whole house needs to obey (unless that's your thing, then I'd highly recommend it). All you need to do is make the habit of stopping, and when people ask you to do something (obviously just as you've sat down) tell them that you're busy. You're busy breathing. Of course, my kids thought I was bonkers at first as I asked them to leave me alone so I could breathe, but now they just know, and they leave me to it. This is the key – asking them to respect what you're doing.

So find a chair, a room in the conservatory, or by the fire or at the kitchen table or in the corner of your bedroom, as I've said, it doesn't matter, and learn to use that space. For you. To sit and be grateful and to breathe - quite literally – deep breaths that will fill your body with oxygen (we're not very good at breathing these days, we breathe very shallowly). Breathe deep into your belly, make it expand so you look pregnant and then pull it back in again. Do that 10 times, 3 times a day and then just sit for a while and contemplate (no, not your navel, just life). You'll be surprised at the changes that will start to happen once you begin to give yourself this breathing space.

"I've got to keep breathing. It'll be my worst business mistake if I don't."
Steve Martin

Niki Schäfer

Creating spaces to relax

When looking at designing any room there are three main questions to ask

- Role – what do you want to do there?
- Character – what do you want it to say about you?
- Setting – how does it work in relation to the other rooms around it and the natural views and light it has already?

Let's look at these questions in the context of creating a relaxing area, a breathing space. Besides the bedroom, where we sleep, our living room is probably the place we relax the most, so I'm going to design this area into being our breathing space. Its role (the first question) is therefore to be a place of relaxation and a space to breathe.

However, the living room is a multi-functional room, it hosts parties, it's where we watch TV, it's where we read and play games, it's where we listen to music and it's where we catch up. And it has to work for all these activities at different times of the day. It's also an incredibly visible room, most often seen by visitors and family so we want to make it look great and have some interesting elements, a feature wall maybe or a unique lamp, for people to notice (even if that person is just us).

243

Breathing space design

The living room can be a complicated room to design or incredibly simple, it all depends on the shape of your room. Those with long thin rooms will appreciate the difficulties and those with beautifully proportioned rooms that centre around a fireplace will not know what I'm referring to. Here is an example of a living room with a relatively simple design layout. The room is in good proportion, there is plenty of light and there is a central focus point.

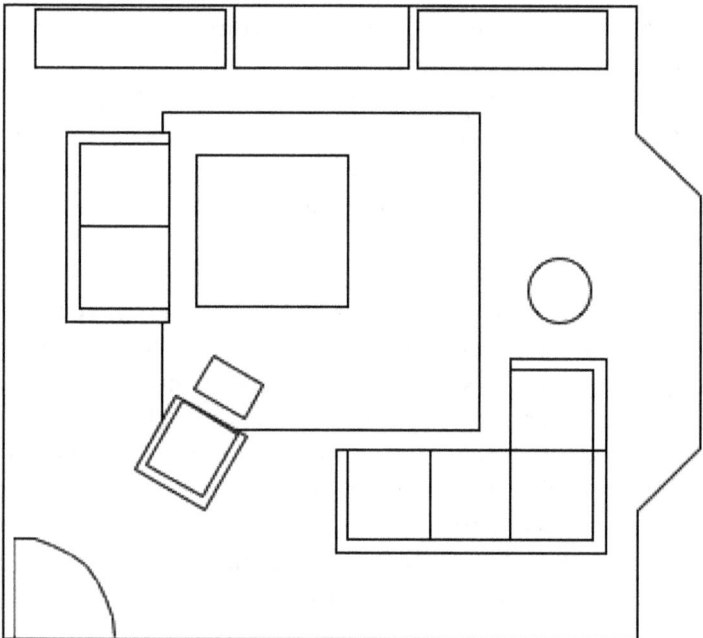

Or perhaps you could work it like this:

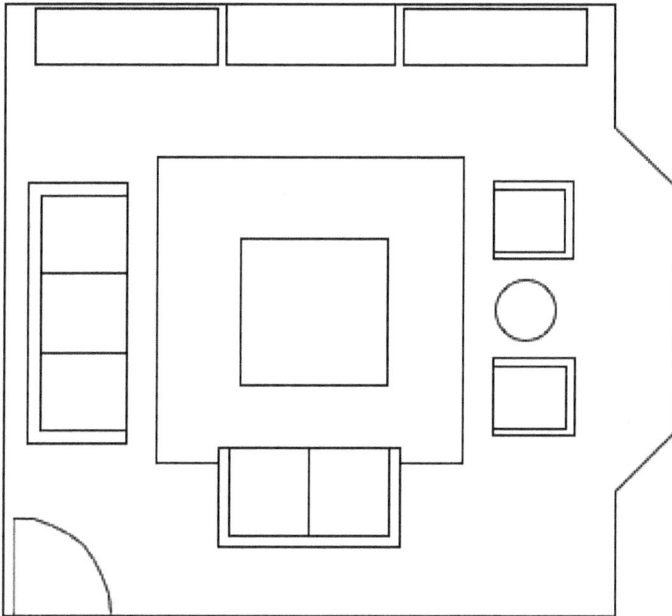

Again the layout is not complicated, it simply reflects a more symmetrical and formal styling. These layouts are straightforward.

Zoning

On the other hand, if you have a long thin room, you're going to have to think a little harder about the layout. This is when 'zoning' can come into play. 'Zoning' is creating areas for different activities. The reading zone, the games zones, the TV zone, the fireplace zone, the storage zone, the central zone, the window zone, the breathing zone. Defining these zones with careful furniture placement, room dividers, or simply rugs, will help people utilise the space properly.

People like to know what a space is supposed to be used for. You can see this very clearly in the body language of people featured in TV property programmes. New home seekers turn up their nose as they wander into a home that has an odd layout, they squint at the 'corridor room' and shake their head, or make funny noises at the living room that feels too big (because it hasn't been zoned properly). The space looks and feels wasted.

Here is an example of how you can lay-out a long thin living room. As you can see there are various different zones to the room. There is a TV, storage unit, rug, coffee table, and various seats in the relaxation zone in front of the window, a desk and bookshelf in the working zone and a dining table and sideboard in the dining zone.

The layout is clear to understand and people know what to do there. (It's a relief, I can't stress this highly enough, we like to know what to do when we get somewhere!)

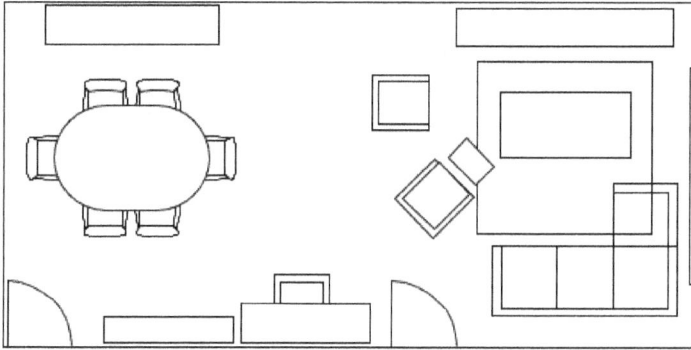

This is what it would look like without the zones.

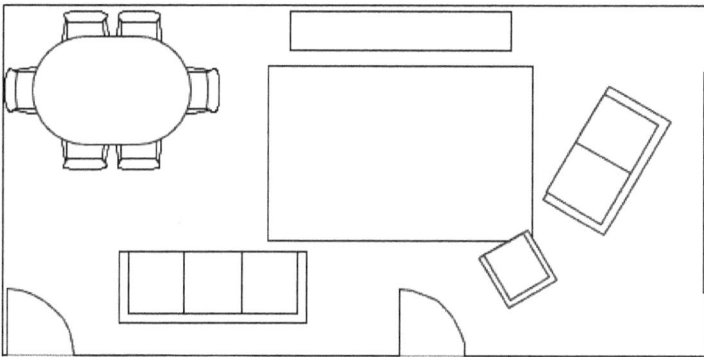

I walk into rooms like this all the time. The door opens straight on to the feature TV in the centre of the wall. There are a variety of large brown leather sofas pushed to the wall perimeters. A rug has been placed centrally, in front of the TV. Despite the large space, the dining table and chairs have been squashed into the corner. There doesn't seem room for an office, so the desk, chair and bookshelf aren't even here. This is frequently what happens when two rooms have been knocked down to create more space. However, the problem is, most people don't know how to use their extra space properly. And as a result, it feels either awkward or like the space is wasted.

Take the time to zone out the different areas of your living room and create space for each activity. This includes the breathing space.

Case study

Laura and Peter had completed extensive building work to their home the year previously. But when we spoke, the walls were still bare and white and there was no carpet. Initially, they were looking for some guidance on how to add some colour but the conversation became considerably more animated between the couple when we started to talk about layout and in particular, which room should be the place for the adults to relax in.

There was a small room off the kitchen at the back of the house, which had little natural light but access to the back garden. Peter wanted to turn this into a warm den, with a 'cosy pub' feel, large armchairs around the fireplace and shelves full of his favourite books.

Laura, on the other hand, saw this area as the children's play room, a space she could close the door on, so she would not see the spilt Lego and the craft projects in mid progress. She had her heart set on the room at the front for the adults. The room, she admitted was small, but full of natural daylight and she felt it was a better space for them to relax together, watch TV and read quietly. The room was painted in a light colour at the time, which they understood maximised the space there.

In these circumstances, there was no easy compromise. One room was to belong to the kids and the other to the adults. I felt that the front room was more suitable to the couple's needs.

However, rather than trying to play tricks with the space, I advised that they paint it a dark warm colour, where they could have the cosy feeling Peter was wanting to achieve in the darker room. The already snug nature of the room would lend itself to a dark green or warm red and adding some thick wool curtains would really create a comforting ambiance. During the day and in the warmer months this décor would still work as the room has sufficient daylight to feel light and airy. It would be a stunning place to sit in the window and breathe with the sun on your back. But in the winter months and the dark nights, it would come into its own.

In the room at the back, I advised we design an area where their young daughters could play (and later) do their homework. I wanted to create a sense of fairy-tale magic to the room so suggested twinkling lights, mirrors, shelf lighting and a light reflective wallpaper on the wall furthest from the window so that it would bounce light back into the room. Combined, these created a real sense of openness and sparkling wonder to the room. And a breathing space that was more an intake of breath in awe at its delicate beauty and connection with the garden outside.

Do you divide adult space from children space in your home?

Colour for breathing space

Once you have decided on a layout for the room, the next step is to find the right scheme. Let's look back at your selected images and see which colours you have chosen as your immediate preferences. Are your images all neutral? Textured wood, a basket of linen, a bowl of eggs, a sandy landscape? Or do they feature colour? A garden filled with wild flowers, a lake with a golden bridge, a cityscape, or a ballerina on stage? There are so many images you could have chosen. Try and separate them into colours. Of your final six, which colours have you chosen?

Neutrals, greens & blues

Traditionally greens and blues are the most relaxing. That's not to say a certain yellow isn't relaxing or even a lilac or pale pink but, on the whole, the blues, greens and the neutrals tend to relax us best. They can quite literally lower our blood pressure and soothe us. The actors 'Green Room' for example, was designed that way so that actors could relax somewhere before they had to go on stage. You'll find that many spas and clinics are decorated using these colours in order to pacify and soothe their clients. They are restful - perhaps they make you think of the sea or, if you prefer, the tranquil greens of a landscape.

You may have chosen electric blue and lime green and if so, I'd recommend using these more vibrant choices in smaller proportions. Greens and blues can also work very well together (especially in a bathroom where the aquatic theme might be most appreciated.) if you dislike blue and green work with the neutral palette and add another accessory colour later if you feel the need. Or stick with neutrals and just go crazy with textures. This is the best way to design using neutrals: always use multiple textures – wool, linen, fur, wood, metal, tiles, silk, fluffy rugs, a textured wallpaper.

In a living room, I'd be inclined to use a neutral base colour and add accessory colours to give the place some colour and life. A neutral base means you can make changes easily (every year or even between seasons) and this flexibility will serve you well over the coming years.

Concept

What is the inspiration for your room? What is your concept? While you could find a perfect blue, green and neutral rug to be the basis for the scheme of your living room, I'd recommend you choose one of the images from your Me Space selection. This will mean your style and the essence of the image you have chosen are truly reflected in the room. This is where Me Space is going to come to life. Your childhood memory of skimming stones at the seaside, the tiered landscape you so loved in Asia, the basket your Grandmother kept logs in, these could be the spirit of your room.

Homework

Choose one of the images you love, an image that is relaxing and peaceful and embodies the type of feeling you want in your living room, the space where you can flop out at the end of the night, read a magazine at the weekend, or do a jigsaw puzzle with your son. Find the image that best fits that type of environment.

Now that you have your relaxing image, look carefully at the details.

Colour

What colours can you really see? Is there just one block of colour or are there several colours merged together? Could you find a fabric that represents those colours? Is this a fabric you could use in the curtaining or the cushions? If the image has a distinct block of colour can you find the perfect paint match? Is this suitable for all four walls or is it more a feature paint, something for the chimney-breast or in the coves behind bookshelves?

If it's a strong colour think about how much of it you'll need in a room. You don't want an over powering presence in a room designed to be relaxing. If it's a strong petrol-blue maybe you could find a vase or a rug that will be noticeable source of colour but won't swamp the room. If it's turquoise then maybe a chair could be upholstered in a fabric of this colour. Or find a piece of art with a splash of turquoise or peacock blue in it.

Examine the other colours – if it's a well-composed image of nature, a photograph maybe, then the colours will likely go together already, without you having to coordinate them. A picture of a bird on a branch will have all the colours you need. All you have to do is use those same colours in the fabrics, the paints and the furniture colours in your room.

Don't make life difficult for yourself. Find a colour you like and then find some complimentary colours that are recommended to you in the paint shop. There are tonnes of sources of colour schemes, some are historic and sludgy, others traditional and bold, more still contemporary and neutral. Coordinating a colour scheme is as simple as that. You don't need a degree in fine art to pick some colours that go well together. (Let one of the paint manufacturers do the hard work for you!)

Proportions

Look at the proportions of the colours in your image. Put a percentage figure to it. How much of your picture is deep green and how much a pale green? How many browns can you see? Now you can duplicate that balance in the scheme of your room. Use the large amount of pale green for the walls, the 10% of dark green for the curtains and the browns in the furniture woods. The rest can be neutral creams and beiges.

If you have a fawn or light grey carpet, a large proportion of your room is already neutrally coloured. Flooring takes up a large percentage of the area of a room. If your image is mostly neutral but has a splash of lime green try adding this colour in a rug. Think also about how much of the room's surface area is taken up with the walls – if you paint them light blue this is the equivalent of a sky background in your image. Add a sandy coloured floor and you've got the beginnings of a beach scene. What colours should your sofas be? Are you bold enough to have a coloured fabric sofa (to represent the deep blue beach hut in your image) or do you stick with neutral and then makes colour changes, as I've suggested, using accessories such as cushions and throws?

Shapes

Look at the shapes in the image you've chosen. Are there straight lines and regimented formality? Or are there gentle curves and swirls that seem to dance in front of your eyes? How can you replicate these shapes in your living room?

A sense of formality can be achieved by placing your furniture and your ornaments in a symmetrical format -- classically the candlestick on either end of the mantelpiece. It can also be seen in how you arrange your seating. Traditional sofas placed facing each other from either side of a fireplace will give a much more formal feel than a curved sofa and asymmetrical arrangement.

Consider your image and look at the level of formality in it. Is it natural and relaxed or more precise? Also think back to the Thinking Space chapter and work out how you think and also how others think. Are the majority of the household formal thinkers and would they like to see this represented in their home? Do you think this would make them feel more comfortable? Would they relax more in a room that has a formal library or organised storage system or in a room that has a more Victoriana feel to it (over stuffed slipper chairs, nick-nacks galore and a set of antlers on the wall)?

Consider your image carefully and see the shapes again. Look at the curves – are they round or is the curve more gentle and flowing – like a river perhaps? If they are round, then consider rounder shapes for your chairs, a tub chair for example or a round-backed chair. If the curves are gentler, replicate this in the chair legs, a sabre leg for example (it looks like the curve of a sword) or consider a more feminine look altogether and look at the French style furniture where curves are hugely celebrated.

If your image is more sturdy and boxy, consider these same shapes for your furniture. Find cube side-tables, or a pyramid chest of drawers. This is a very stable shape, base firmly on the floor (does it remind you of anyone you know?) Or if the opposite applies, then consider a hanging bubble chair (a clear, acrylic bubble that hangs from the ceiling), does this better represent the family way of thinking?

Summary

Use your image as the basis for the decorative scheme:
- Colour and texture – find paint colours that match, or wallpaper that resembles the patterns or the texture in the picture.
- Proportions – if there's a splash of turquoise blue that looks to be about 3% of the image in total use that colour for a cushion or two. If it takes up 15% of the image consider a rug in that colour. If it's the majority of the image (75%) then use this colour as the basis for the walls and even the floor (especially if it's a neutral colour).
- Furniture shapes – replicate the lines in the image with the lines in the furniture – find curved tables for a curvilinear image or a square or rectangular table for a rectilinear image.

Lighting

The lighting in a room can change both the look and feel with the switch of a button. Moods are easily shifted by dimming the lights (or by turning them on again suddenly). As we have previously noted the living room is a room of many moods. It is quiet and calm one moment and set for a party the next. Let's look at how we can achieve a calming effect using light.

There are several different types of lighting:
- General – the down-lights overhead or the pendant in the middle of the room.
- Task lighting – lighting designed for specific roles (e.g. reading).

- Accent lighting – lighting that highlights certain features (e.g. a piece of art or a sculpture).
- Decorative lighting – the pretty stuff (e.g. a chandelier or a funky pendant).
- Architectural or concealed lighting – this is where the real magic happens with lighting, it's the carefully lit walkway up the stairs or the ring of light that appears over a sculpture or the lights that shoot up a column or wash across a wall.

Simple lighting solution

The simplest way to have control over lighting is to put a dimmer switch in. This alone can set an ambiance for a calmer environment.

More advanced lighting solutions

Overhead lighting is very harsh even when dimmed so the best solutions come by mixing up the lighting types as I've described above.

- Use table lamps and standard lamps, which will cast light up and across walls and in the pool directly around them.
- Try picture lights (they're prettier than they used to be) and use them as the sole source of light in the room so the art is spot lit but the room feels quite dark and relaxing. This works especially well when watching TV at night.
- Place down-lights very close to a wall rather than bang in the middle of the room and pick up the texture in the wallpaper or the colours in the curtain fabrics.

Lighting is a specialist subject and requires a trained electrician to install it, but there are so many fabulous ideas that can be achieved if you think through your lighting needs carefully.

Think:

- What do I want to be in the spotlight? (A piece of art, a display unit?)
- What do I want to avoid looking at? (The boxes on top of the cupboard).
- Where do I sit and read or do work that requires a strong direct light?
- What level of light do I want when watching TV?
- What level of light do I want when cleaning the floor?
- What lights bounce off the TV screen – can they be better placed?
- What architectural features are there to highlight – a rose in the ceiling, a niche in the wall?
- Do I want to shine a light across the amazing floor surface (gorgeous tiles or parquet)?
- Do I want the luxury of having a lighting system that can change the mood of the room at the touch of a button? (Or is the TV remote control still a mystery?)

Natural light

Making the most of natural light is one of the fundamental principles of designing any room or home. Humans are instinctively drawn to the lightest part of a room (unless we are hiding something – including ourselves) and we feel better when we are in a good source of light. Placing furniture in the sunspot will have great benefits to you. Sitting quietly with the morning sun on your back is a real pleasure and it's often difficult to pull yourself out of the chair and back into real life. Don't you deserve to have a space like that where you can sit and breathe for a while and be grateful for what you have? A place of peace, tranquillity and calm, no matter how old you are and what your lifestyle is?

Case study

The stairwell in Jenny and Dave's home overlooks the roof of their garage. It's not an exciting view and they are, as a result, not inclined to linger on their way down the stairs.

As we discussed the breathing space of their home I suggested that they consider some kind of a display on the garage roof. It would give them a brief moment of pause on their way down to start the day. I thought something that could make them smile. It would have to be something robust as access was limited to the roof but a shrub display seemed too obvious a choice. A more bespoke option was to think of using the spare bits of bicycles that Dave has in his garage and give them to a 'recycling artist' to create something memorable out of the old bikes. Both Dave and Jenny are passionate about sport and mountain biking and a sculpture seems a fitting way to bring some personality and humour to their 'art'.

If you were to have a sculpture made what would it be of?

Alternative breathing spaces

Creating an environment to help you calm down is, as we have discussed, fundamental. We deserve to walk through the door and breathe a huge sigh of relief. If not, we're likely to turn around and walk straight back out again. If this is the case, let's make sure it's our back door we walk out of and head straight into our garden.

Gardens are one of the most relaxing spaces in your home and being in nature can have an enormous impact on your health and well-being. If you're not a big gardener though (or secretly think it's only for the retired) then why don't you consider bringing some of that outdoor goodness indoors?

Having plants around your home will bring oxygen and life into the space. Most houseplants are incredibly easy to look after. As long as they have a bit of water, sunshine and the occasional supply of nutrients they'll be there for you year in year out. Looking after plants is cathartic and as good for you as it is for the plants. Spending time to slow down and see what the plant needs is in itself a form of meditation and 'breathing space'.

The literal sense of a breathing space is also important and having the right kind of ventilation in a home is necessary for both health and safety reasons. Allowing the room to breathe, for odours to leave and fresh air to come into the room is as common sense as opening a window. On the other hand, if there's a fire in the room then there are regulations that need to be followed.

Bathroom

Another alternative breathing space is the bathroom. Not the hectic version in the morning when elbows are swinging and queues outside are forming but on a weekend afternoon or an evening. It is then that warm bubbles can soothe or the rain shower can wash away the troubles. Making this room into a haven of relaxation can be as simple as lighting candles and removing the bath toys or more sophisticated by bringing in some ideas that soothe. Perhaps from the outside – use pebbles to simulate a beach or reeds and grasses in an acrylic shower panel. Also consider painting the ceiling a warm colour. This has the effect of bringing the ceiling closer and giving a more cosy feeling which can really work when you're lying in the bath. Breathing.

Bathroom design is frequently an exercise in how to maximise the small space available. Careful planning and design is required for this room and for those even smaller rooms, the downstairs loo, be it in a room of its own, hidden under the stairs or tucked in with the washing machine, the tumble dryer and every coat and Wellington boot you and the kids have ever owned. Here are some space-saving tips (to allow you a little breathing space) and other bathroom tricks.

- Consider carefully the swing of the door. Would opening the door into the corridor save you sacred space inside the room?
- A sliding door is another option.
- Bear in mind where the service pipes are. (Especially if you're creating a new bathroom or adding an en-suite). Keep pipes close together and preferably at the rear of the house.
- Boxing in pipe work removes the unsightly 'behind-the scenes' aspect of the bathroom and can also lead to storage ideas.
- Use every nook and cranny for storage. You'll find bottles and towels fit in neatly.
- If you're building walls (e.g. a shower wall and room divider) make it wide enough to incorporate niches for shampoo bottles (beats them sitting on the shower floor or those hideous corner hanging units).
- Speaking of hideous, please avoid shower curtains. They rot and smell and look terrible after about three months and will need replacing. A screen is, in the long run, actually cheaper.
- Adjusting floor levels can create much-needed space in a bathroom (a sunken bath or even shower).
- Always, always have easy access to the plumbing. Sod's Law says something will go wrong if you don't.
- If you have roof eaves to contend with, bear in mind the shower needs to be in the highest part of the room. This is obvious in elevation (wall) drawings but is frequently overseen in plan (layouts).
- Always position your shower controls in a spot where your hand won't get wet to turn them on. (Very annoying!)

- If you are thinking about having a bath in your bedroom (very hotel chic!), bear in mind that the room needs to be very large. A comfortable temperature to bathe in is 23 degrees, however we sleep much better at 19 degrees or below. If you have an evening bath and then head to bed, you'll be sticky and uncomfortable if the room isn't large enough to dissipate the heat.
- Make sure there's a window in your bathroom or toilet. The extractor fans today are marvellous, but nothing beats opening the window. And natural light is beneficial to your well-being, even in this room.
- Decorate your loo with lots of fabulous photographs. Give people a reason to justify how long they spend in there.
- Decorate your loo in your wildest possible taste. You don't spend a huge amount of time in there and it will tickle you pink every time you pay a visit. Make yourself laugh. (This is the kind of toilet humour I actually appreciate.)

The art of breathing

As I've said, we don't breathe very well these days. When asked to take a deep breath, we puff up our chests like chickens and fill our lungs with air but this only gives us a small proportion of the oxygen we so crucially need for our bodies. We need to think a little lower and fill up our bellies if we want to truly maximise our breathing. This is diaphragmatic breathing and is what you learn in yoga, in acting and singing classes, and also personal development and life coaching seminars (because it's a life skill). The power of breathing is so fundamental to our health and happiness yet somehow we think it's a bit obvious to really spend the time cultivating the art of breathing.

Take the time now to breathe properly. Focus your attention on one of the ideas you've been developing for your home be it the perfect colour for your living room or simply the idea of creating a calmer home.

Take a deep breath in through your nose and hold it deep in your diaphragm (your belly should stick out... I know, it's the last thing we need, but really no one is watching). Then exhale slowly through your mouth. Do this a couple of times to get into the practice of filling your belly (if your shoulders are shooting up to your ears, you're doing this wrong. Your chest should fill once your diaphragm is full but it should not move excessively).

Breathing pattern

Work to the following ratio: 1:4:2 inhale for 1, hold the breath for 4 and exhale for 2. Start by inhaling for 4 seconds, holding for 16 seconds and exhaling for 8 seconds. As you progress you'll be able to last a little longer, perhaps 7 seconds to inhale, 28 seconds to hold and 14 seconds to exhale.

The idea isn't to hold your breath until you pass out, it's to train your lungs to take in sufficient oxygen. So do this comfortably. Breathing is an art not a competition and should be enjoyed. Think of something beautiful or something you are grateful for while you are doing this exercise. Try imagining something in the future that you'd really like to be grateful for (that your husband takes out the bins without you nagging him? That your daughter does her homework without needing a prompt or that your son tides up his room? Or think a little bigger.)

When breathing, find somewhere you can feel the warmth and the light of the sun. Intentionally absorb its energy. Focus on the sun (not by looking directly at it, obviously, just by soaking up its rays), focus on what you're grateful for, start the breathing and then slowly let go of anything that is going on in your mind except for your breath. As you exhale let go of the tension and the worries and smile.

Repeat the breathing pattern ten times. Do this two or three times a day. Create the time to do this (you know how). It's a great practice and will help you to enjoy your holidays and other relaxation time more. Many people find it very difficult to wind down and can waste days of their holiday still thinking about work and the things they have still to do. This practice will help you to build a habit of relaxation so that you can see its benefits and implement them whenever it suits you. It beats being ill on holiday which is what happens when you're not in the habit and your body simply caves in once the adrenaline has gone.

Homework overview

- Start a gratitude diary.
- Consider the design layout for your living room.
- Develop a decorative scheme.

- o Look at your image selection – find the calming images.
- o Take note of the colours and shapes in these images.
- o Replicate these in the colour scheme and the furniture designs.
- Have an understanding of your lighting needs.
- Learn the breathing pattern and establish a time to breathe in your day.

Congratulations

You have travelled through the sixth space of your home and are now able to create a scheme for somewhere to sit and breathe. You have the skills to be able to take inspiration from an image and turn it into a basic decorative scheme using colours and shapes and an understanding of proportions. These are incredibly useful design skills.

Consider now whether your living room is the space you would like to have as your place of relaxation or whether a garden room (or conservatory) or bathroom is more appropriate. We have focussed on the living area but breathing is such an important aspect of your life that I'd recommend you do it everywhere!

In the next chapter we will look at the heart space, the centre of the home, where our families eat, play and talk together. I've left it until last because it is such an important space and it will have a wonderful impact on your family life when you get this space right. We'll also take the last step of creating a decorative scheme. You are almost home.

"The essence of all beautiful art, all great art, is gratitude."
Friedrich Nietzsche

FOUNDATION 2: FAMILY THINKING

Space 7 - Heart Space

"The best and most beautiful things in the world cannot be seen or even touched - they must be felt with the heart."
Helen Keller

DWELL-BEING MODEL

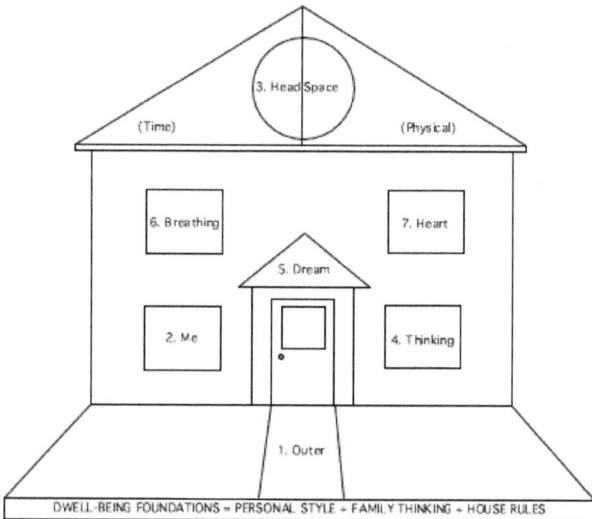

3. Head Space

(Time)   (Physical)

6. Breathing   7. Heart

5. Dream

2. Me   4. Thinking

1. Outer

DWELL-BEING FOUNDATIONS = PERSONAL STYLE + FAMILY THINKING + HOUSE RULES

Outer Space
o   You know what home means.
o   Your home has a warm welcome.

Me Space
o   You know your own taste.
o   You know your own mind.

Head Space
o   You have your own space.
o   You have your own time.

Thinking Space
o   You respect others.

Dream Space
o   You can design bedrooms.
o   You know how to succeed in your goals.

Breathing Space
o   You can design a place to relax.
o   You are grateful.

In **Heart Space** you will learn to:
o   Organise and decorate places to eat and be together.
o   Build a space to feel, to listen, to be heard and to be loved.

Conclusion
o   House rules – dos and don'ts.
o   Housekeeping exercises.

Heart space chapter outcome

By the end of this chapter you will:
- Understand the centre of your home.
- Know how to design a cooking and dining area where your family can connect.
- Never underestimate again the importance of feeling heard and understood.

- Be able to develop a complete decorative scheme from your images.

Home truth

Your husband walks in after a day at work and heads straight for the fridge. He throws together a hurried dinner and then settles down in front of the news to eat his food and let the events at work fade and merge with those across the world. After much insistence, the kids put away their various consoles and, following several failed distraction tactics (sore tummy, need another glass of water etc.), they begrudgingly go to bed. You had grabbed a meal with the kids earlier but think you might feel hungry enough for a yoghurt (or a small bar of chocolate) and so finally, after cleaning the kitchen and preparing the bags for tomorrow's clubs, you settle down on the sofa to discuss your day and tell him any gossip you picked up since you last saw him. Only he's not listening because he's fast asleep. "It's Friday night, things sure didn't use to be this way," you think as you close your eyes and join him.

What is the heart of the home?

We are spending less time eating together and talking to one another. We eat while watching TV, we text while eating, while watching TV. The heart of the home that once was a fireplace is now very firmly a large black screen and the time we once spent talking around that fire is now dedicated to arguing over who has control of the remote.

Niki Schäfer

Much like the heart in a body, the heart of a home is the engine room. It is the centre of the house where we gather together, where issues are discussed, where tea is brewed, where problems are shared, where homework is done, where businesses are started, where shoulders are cried on, where toast is burnt. The heart of the home is where we fuel ourselves, our bodies with the food from the kitchen and our souls with the stories from our lives.

Open plan

The kitchen was always the source of fire and fuel and the centre of gossip in a house. As we all know it's the best place to be at parties and it's the same at breakfast. It's a place to see the lay of the land, a room to check out who's doing what and why. Today, however, it's not so much a room as a central space and is probably the hardest working space in the house – much like the heart is to the body.

Unless you like to work in private and have the kitchen to yourself, the kitchen is fast becoming a far more open plan area than it once was. Industrial strength extractor fans mean we no longer have the lingering smell issues associated with cooking and so this area merges very nicely with the family play area and the dining room. These three rooms are a powerhouse of communication and entertainment. They are truly the heart of the home.

Needs

What does the heart of the home need? Think about the heart of a space, what does that convey to you? What

271

does it mean? Here are some answers you might consider:

- A source of energy (be it food or just good vibes).
- A place to enjoy the company of others.
- A space to share stories, problems or achievements.
- A place to be heard (not because you've raised your voice).
- A place to feel loved (adored, enjoyed, appreciated, admired, go wild!)
- A place to feed yourself, and others, well.
- A hardworking environment.
- A space of respect (you and others).

Now, you may well be wondering whether it's even possible to design a place where you feel heard and you respect others. You might think that more likely for a church or other place of worship. But I believe we can create these environments at home (and there's no need for pews and an altar, just a kitchen bench and an Aga).

Relationships in the house

In Thinking Space we talked at length about how different members of the house think differently and, with luck, you have noticed this and made changes to accommodate the thinking patterns of your partner and children. Have your relationships changed as a result?

Now we've understood that we all behave and think differently there is a very simple way of ensuring a harmonious relationship with all members of your household. Would you like to know the secret? It's not as difficult as you may imagine, in fact it's very easy. You simply give them what they need. No, I'm not talking about mindlessly handing over another 3DS game or giving them chocolate cereal every morning just because they want it. These will make them happy but it will be a short-lived happiness. I'm talking about finding solutions that will bring them genuine fulfilment in the long run. And this requires not just giving them what they want but giving them what they really need.

Wants and needs

The secret to building positive relationships in the home is about understanding the needs of others. And figuring out what others genuinely *need* requires a more advanced approach than asking outright what they *want* and expecting a well-formed response. It requires active listening and heartfelt understanding.

Active listening is not listening while texting or watching the TV or even while cooking dinner. It's also not listening and just waiting to jump in with the obvious solution that *you've* known all along.

Active listening is:
- Asking open-ended questions and allowing them to talk freely. (No butting in).
- Watching *how* they respond, as well as listening to the words they speak. (Rely on your intuition more, you can see when someone is hurting or when they're trying to cover something up, can't you?)

- Empathising with the emotions they are going through but not being dragged into their pain (if the conversation is in fact painful).
- Waiting until they have finished speaking until you give any solutions or ideas. (Or simply remaining quiet and letting silence do the good work.)
- Two ears and one mouth (and using them in that proportion).

For a home to be happy it needs a healthy and well-designed heart space - a place where we build our relationships with others, where we find out their needs and figure out how we can meet them.

Heartfelt understanding

Heartfelt understanding is about getting to the bottom of someone else's needs. It's respecting that these needs may be different to our own and yet still appreciating that they are as important as ours. Frequently, when we see others in need, we overlay *our* needs and *our* ways of behaving on to them. And while we are doing our best, trying to help them in a way that we would want to be helped, sometimes it just doesn't work. Sometimes our efforts are re-buffed or ignored and this can be painful for us too. So what can we do to help more effectively?

It helps to have an understanding of our basic human needs. This will help you interpret the behaviour of others (as well as your own). Once you have an appreciation of how other people are trying to meet their needs you can help them much easier. You can see how their actions are supporting their needs. (And you'll appreciate that some of these actions are more harmful than they are helpful.)

Human needs - what do you need?

In Outer Space we looked at Maslow's human needs in order to assess how they relate to our home. Now we will look again at the human needs as defined by Tony Robbins. He teaches us that each and every one of us, no matter which country we come from, our upbringing or our age, have the following six human needs:

1. **Certainty.** The first need is for certainty. We need to feel sure. This will bring with it a sense of security and strength.
   - How do you feel when you *know* something? Do you feel solid? Do you feel safe? Is this a comforting feeling?
   - We save money in order to feel safe in our future. We get jobs to feel secure. We also eat certain types of food to feel secure. (Shepherd's pie with a mountain of peas, or is a chicken balti more up your comfort food street?)
   - We stick with what we know, and often put up with old habits out of a sense of security and comfort. Are there any old habits you have that you're relying on for the sense of familiarity rather than what it is truly doing for you? (While this question is stuck in the middle here, it really is a bit of a biggy. Give it some careful consideration.)

- Equally we are loyal and true to our family, friends and country because we feel certain about them.
- Our homes are a great source of certainty, security and strength.

2. **Uncertainty/variety.** The second need is in direct conflict with the first and that is our need for uncertainty. If we were sure of everything all the time, then we'd be bored. We therefore need a sense of variety and interest.
   - We go to the gym to feel different. We put music on to feel different. We pick a fight to feel different.
   - We send sweet 'I love you' texts at random times of the day. We organise surprise parties. We put treats into their packed lunches to make them smile.
   - Variety is the spice of life and it can be as addictive as any other need. The need for newness. Newness is exciting and unpredictable.
   - Do you like surprises? Do you like to try new things? Do you eat just to feel different? (I do this all the time. It's the reason my thighs are the way my thighs are.)
   - How we decorate our home can be a source of variety and surprise, especially for parties and Christmas.

3. **Significance.** We have a need for significance. We need to feel important. This isn't always about

kudos and fame, this is equally about the need to simply be needed.

- How do you want to be needed? Do you like to hear your name being called? Do you secretly love the sound of 'Muuuuummmm' being yelled through the house? Do you like flocks of people around you? Do you like a full inbox?

- Our need to be needed expresses itself in many different ways. We share our problems so that people give us the sympathy and attention we need. We show off. We point out the faults of others so we feel better about ourselves.

- We go for promotions so we can have a better title and more recognition. We compete for awards. We love medals.

- On the other hand, we build self-esteem, we know ourselves well, we recognise our own self-worth because we *are* significant.

- Our homes are a significant part of our lives. They are the stage on which much of our life story is performed.

4. **Love.** We have a need for connection and for love. We want to belong with others and to feel the bond between us. This can be intimate love or can be belonging to a book club. We need a sense that we are part of a group.

  - How do you feel when you feel bonded? How can you tell the difference between a simple chat and a conversation when you are truly connected?

- Our need for love is at the heart of most songs, books and movies and is a feeling we all know. We yearn for love, we are jubilant when we find love, and we are despondent when we lose it. It is at our core.
- Some would say God is love and others would say love is just a chemical reaction.
- I've read that love is one human being positively responding to another because they express the traits that we love in ourselves. (I like to point this out to my husband, as I gaze lovingly at him and tell him how fabulous I am… It's important to have a sense of humour about this I find!)
- What do you do in the name of love? (No small question, I can assure you).
- Your home is possibly the most important environment of love of them all. Where else do you connect and express love as much? (If the answer is your local disco on a Friday night then I can only congratulate you for getting this far into the book and wanting to make such a radical change!)

5. **Growth.** The fifth need is a need for growth. We need to go beyond ourselves and learn. We need to develop and improve. Tony Robbins calls this and the following need our spiritual needs (where the first four were human needs). They represent the needs of our more developed selves.
   - Growing is about learning. It's about educating ourselves and learning the lessons from our own experiences.

- What are your areas of interest? How would you like to develop? This needn't mean an evening course at the local college, it could simply come from reading or from deciding to be a better parent and doing your utmost to grow into that.
- The sensation of learning and developing can again be as addictive as any other need (don't you know a course junkie or two?), so make sure you're heading in the right direction.
- Let your home be a source of stimulation for interesting ideas and equally of support to help you grow.

6. **Contribution.** The final need is of contribution. We have a need to give to others, to help others and to pay back.
   - We contribute our time – to our family, to our community, to our friends.
   - We contribute financially – to charities and to local needs.
   - We contribute our experience - by helping others who need a hand.
   - We contribute our energy – by being there for people.
   - We contribute our wisdom – by teaching, by leading, by showing the way.
   - We contribute our home – by inviting others into it.
   - How do you want to contribute?

Calm, sane environment

Creating an environment where you can achieve these needs is how to create a calm and sane home. Designing areas where we listen actively and where we are in a position to use our heartfelt understanding are the keys. While private conversations that take places in bedrooms are, of course, absolutely necessary, I think that the informal kitchen table (or the slightly more formal dining table) are the places for these conversations to start. They are the places we should notice others, where we can hear them and where we can assess their needs, on a daily (or if not, at least weekly) basis. This is what heart space is.

How often do you eat together?

I applaud you if you are a family who sit and eat a meal together on a daily basis. If you can share the details of your day with someone else you are in a privileged position. If you can listen to the tales of woe and equally the magnificent achievements your children have accomplished then they are extremely fortunate. We live in a time when our children don't need more presents but need more of our presence. To be truly present means they feel heard and they feel understood.

Isn't this the same for you? How do you feel when you feel sincerely heard? When someone, be it a friend, family member or even a stranger, has taken the time to listen to you and to empathise with how you feel. It's as if a burden has been lifted.

Or, if you're not a sharer of facts and personal details, don't you simply feel better for the pleasure of having someone by your side, to enjoy the food with? Isn't this the very purpose of marriage and having a family?

Why then do we insist on having a better relationship with technological products? (I call her the iWife... but I'm pleased to say she's not as shapely as I am!) Understanding how your partner and your children think, then going out of your way to meet their needs, can be as much fun as it is deeply rewarding and extraordinarily beneficial for that relationship.

Instead of moaning about what's going on (not to suggest that you would, obviously), use your abilities to listen actively, investigate which of their needs are being met, and then act accordingly. For example, your daughter is yo-yoing between friendships at school and is confused about who her real friends are. She wants to feel certain and she also wants to feel connected but new exciting additions to the playground are frequently tempting (the need for uncertainty). How can you help her meet all these needs without affecting her friendships? How can she feel certain that she is loved by her friends but can also meet new people? Can you set up a club for her to attend where there are new people for her to meet, for example?

You might like to also consider your own needs, as you think about what you want to do once the children are all at school. Is this an opportunity for you to find work or would you like to have some time to yourself, to focus on some personal (or corporate) development? You want to feel certain that the family is safe and secure, of course, and you're always at home for them (just in case) but you might also need a bit of variety, some adventure even. Have you considered setting up a business of your own? Will this bring you certainty? (For the record, that's not very likely, but it will be exciting and will supply you with variety in spades.) It's time to discover your own needs and find out how to meet them.

Your husband's needs are also a factor. I suspect he spends a lot of his day being very significance driven. In a working world, men have to prove themselves to one another (I won't go as far as to call it chest beating but...) and when they return home, they need to feel certain - certain that they are loved, certain that they are doing the right thing for their family, certain that they are providing. How often do you tell your partner how grateful you are for what they provide? How often do you 'big them up' to simply make them feel good about themselves? How often do you let them be 'the man'? Or do you just hand them the screaming baby and say 'It's about time you're home, it's been horrible here and I need a break'?

Have you considered the idea of giving him a half hour of 'breathing space' followed by a few well-chosen words of gratitude (to meet his significance and certainty needs) followed by a suggestion of love and connection (once the kids have gone to bed), all of which might just bring about his 'variety need', and he might just offer to take the kids off your hands for a while so you can go and have a catch up on the phone (or in the bath, or down the shops, or at the gym?) It's worth a try, surely.

Homework

Consider a situation in your family right now. Think about the people involved and how they are meeting their needs.

- What certainty needs are they/ you meeting?
- What variety are they seeking?
- What level of significance is involved?
- What love or connection is trying to be met?
- How are they/ you growing by being involved in this situation? (And is it growth in the right direction?)
- Is there any contribution?

Understanding the needs involved will automatically give you a much better comprehension of what is going on and will lead you to some conclusions and resolutions you hadn't previously considered. Write down your thoughts.

Fun

You'll be relieved to hear that 'good' conversation needn't always be deep and meaningful. Entertainment works just as well. As I've mentioned in a previous chapter, it's the oxytocin that makes us happy. (Oxytocin is the feel good chemical that's released when you're looking into someone's eyes). So start entertaining. It could be as simple as inviting a few friends over and having a coffee or you could push the boat out and have a dinner party.

The only problem is that most of us are a little embarrassed by the state of our houses. We don't want to invite people over for fear of what they might think of our homes. The dreaded silence as someone looks around your home can be painful. Feeling judged isn't fun.

The plethora of interior design shows has contributed to this nicely, leaving the feeling that all homes should be show homes these days. But this need to be perfect is just a myth. Perfection is not attainable and the energy we consume in trying, and failing, to get there will be a lifetime wasted. Leave perfection out of it and just design somewhere that you love. Everyone will feel that far more than they would the fake (or intimidating) feeling of perfection.

Designing social spaces

What does your kitchen/ dining/ family space look like? Is it three rooms (or two) that you'd like to knock into one or are you happy having separate spaces? Is your kitchen integral to this area or is it in a closed off part of the house? Is that how you like to work or would you prefer the company of others as you create your culinary delights? Is there a family space at all in this part of your house where kids can watch their TV or do their homework under your watchful gaze? Do you have a sofa positioned perfectly in the morning light where you can sit around in your PJs eating your cornflakes? (A little slice of heaven before the day begins in earnest).

Niki Schäfer

And what about more formal dining? Do you have a separate dining room? Is it used frequently, or just for high days and holidays? Can you afford to lose that space to a room only used so occasionally? Would you consider knocking down a wall so that the dining table also plays the role of the kitchen table or does the idea of looking at dirty dishes and thinking you need to wash them up before you eat put you off your food? Because there are lighting solutions to that problem you know.

Heart space

The kitchen, dining room, family room is a bit of a mouthful, so I will call it the heart space from now on. Let's look at it from a design perspective, as we would do any other room. Remember the three fundamental questions:

1. What role does this room play?
    a. What do you want to do in this space?
    b. How does it feature in your day?
    c. What do you not want to do there?
    d. What do you want to feel, see, hear or not hear there?
2. What is the character of this space?
    a. What do you want it to say about you?
    b. What inspires you about it?
    c. What similar 'heart spaces' do you admire?
    d. What 'heart spaces' do you remember?
3. What is the setting of this space?
    a. What is the orientation? Which way is the space facing (North, South, East or West?)

    b. Which other rooms are positioned around this room?

    c. What are the views from the windows?

    d. What is the natural lighting like in this space?

    e. What is the architectural styling of this room?

The answers to these questions will give us a guideline as to how to design the space. I've broken them down in more detail below. The list of thoughts and questions is not extensive but it will give you some considerations to mull over and some potential ideas to ponder.

Role

- The role of this space is to cook, eat and be sociable with family and friends. Additional roles might also be relaxation, homework and working from home.

- It is likely to be used heavily in the morning and in the evening when breakfast and dinners are prepared, school days are organised and homework is done. During the day time spent here will obviously depend on whether people are home or not.

- We have discussed how we want to feel here at length – this is a place of understanding. It is also a place of meeting needs be they the fundamentals of being fed or the more complex needs of personal growth. This is the place we discuss how we feel. (Where else would the conversation about which school to go to take place?)

Character

- What do you want it to say about you? We have examined your personal style in Me Space and we have also taken into consideration the style of others in Thinking Space. Heart Space is definitely a space where a consensus must be met. It is a space for all and everyone needs to feel comfortable and welcomed here.
- It is also a place where we would like to encourage social engagement and this will have an impact on our decorative choices (I'll explain shortly).
- Have you been in any heart spaces that you'd love to see in your own home? Have you visited a house where the layout was something you'd like to replicate? Have you seen any on the TV? (Bear in mind that TV soap sets are not real rooms and have only two walls, so will always feel more spacious than a real room with four!).
- From a farmhouse kitchen to a high-tech communication hub there are many sources of inspiration for the look and feel of your heart space.

Setting

- The orientation of the building will dictate which way the rooms are facing which in turn will predict the amount of natural light in the room. A space for breakfasting is served well by the morning light from the East. Is there a portion of this area where this heartening warm light can be captured?

- What are the windows like in this space? Would a roof light that opens the space up to the sky, or bi-fold doors, which do likewise to the garden, make the world of difference? It is simple decisions like these that can make profound changes to how you live your life.

- What is the architectural style of this area of your home? Is it a modern box you can change with ease or do you have regulations to handle?

- And what of the other rooms around this space – will they have an impact on its layout? Where should the utility room be? Do you want the washing machine and tumble dryer in this area or would it make sense to have them upstairs near the laundry? (Finally a design decision that'll save you schlepping up and down the stairs with baskets and baskets of clothes).

Heart space rooms

The heart space is made up of three rooms: the kitchen, the dining room and the family room. Here are the design considerations, some layout tips and some decorative suggestions for this area.

Kitchen

Designing a kitchen is a highly specialised field. Do it properly. Get an expert in. It will make a difference on a daily basis if you have a room that works for you (as opposed to a hindrance to you) and compliments your personal working style. While you think a couple of paces across the room to reach something you need isn't a 'big deal', this will not be the case when you have small children underfoot or ten hungry people at the table waiting. While you have the chance design it into how you want it. Don't compromise here.

Spend some time thinking about how you work in your kitchen, what your favourite dishes are to cook, which your favourite implements and tools are to use. Look at how you move around your kitchen. Are you smooth and efficient or are you back and forth like a yo-yo? Write down your thoughts and then speak with a specialist kitchen designer (and then don't let them off the hook until it works brilliantly for you.)

Obviously, you also have to bear in mind that the kitchen needs to work for your partner too, so make sure he's involved in the process, or he'll never want to work alongside you again. (I'll let you figure out whether this is good news, or not).

When it comes to decorating this part of the house, you can really make a statement. Kitchens are unique in their styling versatility because a super contemporary kitchen in an early Georgian mansion will not look out of place and nor will a country kitchen seem inappropriate in a modern house. (The same cannot be said for an early Georgian dining room in a red brick semi.)

So, if you want this room to feel different, you can. However, if it's open-plan and part of the heart space, I'd recommend you create a cohesive scheme for the entire area and we will be looking at these ideas shortly.

Dining room

The dining room is such a simple room. It requires a table, some chairs, a great light, a bit of storage and good access to the kitchen. Don't mess this up. Don't over complicate this space. Having said that, do bear in mind what your guests will be looking at. Make sure you haven't got the dishwasher in plain view. Consider a window instead.

Family area

Be it an L-shaped sofa with table, TV and its own lighting system or a breakfast bar and high stool the 'family area' is where the chef's friends can perch with a glass of white wine or the kids can do their thing while the cook prepares dinner. It is generally an informal part of the 'heart space' and should be designed with comfort in mind. (When you're basting the turkey on Christmas Eve this is the space you want your mother-in-law to be in, sherry in hand and definitely out from under your feet.)

Heart space layout

There are multiple layout possibilities for this area and they depend hugely on the architectural layout of the house. Some good working practice however would be:

- Figure out the best light – this is a priority spot – what deserves to go there?
- Design your kitchen with your working style in mind – give this some serious consideration as it might be with you for 10 years!
- Have the seating area with a view into the garden.
- Ensure there is good flow between these spaces but don't just create one big open space - zone the space and make sure each zone has interesting elements to it.

Heart space decoration

Developing a decorative scheme for the heart space is the same principle as we have followed for every other space, (except with perhaps a few more functional considerations when it comes to choosing appropriate materials for the kitchen.) Here are some guidelines on material choices:

- Aluminium scratches (it looks great for the celebrity TV chef, but it'll drive you insane).
- Glass scratches (use it only as a splash back – also consider something pretty to go behind it – art or mosaics perhaps?)
- If you're going to use limestone, buy good quality and seal it properly otherwise it will soak up any spillages (including red wine).
- Bear grease and dirt in mind when thinking about fabrics for windows in the kitchen. (This also applies to highly decorative light fittings). Silk is an absolute no-no.

- Keep your materials palette limited (probably only 3), the kitchen is a busy room already, it doesn't need to feel fussy by too many shiny granites competing for your attention (when you should be focussing on the pan boiling).

Let's go back to the images you chose in Me Space and create a scheme from there. Do you have the six images? Have a look at them and see which of them best represents this space? Are there any images with lots of people? Any social environments? Is there an informal picture that suits this space? What colours have you chosen? Which shapes? Which of these colours and shapes looks more inviting? Which of them are warm and welcoming?

Reds, oranges and yellows

Where blues and greens were calm and soothing colours, reds and oranges are at the warmer end of the spectrum (you don't need an interior designer to tell you that). What you might not know is that red and orange are so effective at 'warming us up' that we are more open and conversation flows better under this colour. As a result they are fabulous colours for dining rooms where we are keen to keep conversation going. Ornaments or 'conversation starters', such as interesting pieces of art or posters, are also indispensable for this room. I like to choose statement pieces of lighting and interesting fabrics for the chairs as well. Dinner parties will flow with ease if there's a fun seat cover to chat about or an amazing pendant overhead.

Let's go back to your images. Choose one or two that best represent the feel of the heart space. Do these images work well together? If they do then we can combine the elements from them. If not then perhaps we can focus on one and use only contrasting aspects from the other. Do either of them have warm colours? Can this be the basis for the colour scheme? It doesn't mean that the walls have to be solid red or bright orange. We could just use these as accent colours but it will definitely enhance the welcoming nature of the room if there are warm colours around.

Choosing fabrics

Which fabrics are required in this area?
- Curtains in the dining room. (Or do you prefer to keep the windows clear?)
- Blinds at the kitchen windows.
- An upholstery fabric or leather for the sofa or kitchen bench.
- Upholstery fabrics for dining chairs.
- Accessory fabrics for cushions and throws, if you have a sofa or armchair in the room.

You might also like to consider the rug as a large source of colour as well. I wouldn't always recommend a rug under a dining or kitchen table but they work well for zoning off each area and will definitely be needed next to a sofa or under a small coffee table (in the family area). A rug can also be the starting point of your decorative scheme. The shapes and colours in it can be the inspiration for the rest of the furniture and fabric choices.

Alternatively use a piece of art as the inspiration or simply work from one of the images you have chosen.

Look at the images again carefully or just squint at them – make them into a mass of lines, curves, colours and patterns. If you break these down then you'll soon see them in other designs. You'll see the shapes of the dining table leg or the curve of the breakfast bar. You can also find fabrics that match your image. They don't have to be picture perfect they just need to resemble the picture. Take your image to your local department store and look in the fabrics department for fabrics that resemble your image.

This is a well-used and taught practice at interior design schools. Inspiration has to come from somewhere and the curve of a shell, or an inherited painting, might as well be it. So take your chosen inspiration and base your decorative scheme on that. Not only will this give you a scheme that you already know works (because you like the picture) it is my opinion that the feelings you have for the image should then fuse their way into the fabric of the room. You should feel the emotion of the images every time you're in the room, even if it's not always consciously.

"Sometimes the heart sees what is invisible to the eye."
H. Jackson Brown Jr.

Details

In Yorkshire there was a carpenter referred to as 'Mouse Man'. He chiselled a small mouse on to all his pieces of woodwork and as a child I had the privilege of sitting in church pews that held these mice. They were not the centre-piece of the church but their presence was felt (and believe me they were a comfort during some rather lengthy sermons on a Sunday morning). Details such as these are so important to a room. They are not the be-all-and-end-all, they are not the conversation starters, they are more intrinsic than that.

I have a friend who writes messages on his furniture. 'Love' and 'hope' are written on the base of his tables. No one knows about them except him (and probably his young children once they're old enough to read) but he knows they're there and, to him, it's a comfort. The room is filled with love and hope because he has decided that this should be the case. I love this idea and it's as meaningful to me as any secret code passed down by the so-called Illuminati in the mystery books, or coats of arms that have such magnificent heritage and historical significance. Why can't we create our own symbols demonstrating our personal and family values? And where better a room to create them for than the heart space?

Messages

What messages does your house give off? We discussed in Outer Space how easily an environment is judged but are there more subtle ways of sending messages to others? Does a room not feel better when it's clean, when it's clear of clutter, when the light is good, when the colours are harmonious? Don't you get the sense of whether a house is happy as you walk up the front path?

And while I've stated earlier that how we tend the garden and look after the skirting boards play a role sometimes a home can look scruffy but still feel very loving and comforting.

What creates such an environment? Is it the homemade art on the wall? Is it the well-worn armchair? Is it the fireplace or the Aga or the screeching of an old fashioned kettle? The truth is that there is no one answer. The answers can only come from you.

Heart space for you will look very different to heart space for me. And neither of us is right or wrong. The ultimate judge is simply whether we feel welcomed and loved in such a space. While the decoration can only contribute minimally to this it does have a role to play if only to remind you to sit and take a break with your friends and your family. Have a chat, find out what they're up to and genuinely listen to what's going on in their lives. This active listening and the heartfelt understanding that comes with it will contribute more significantly to the happiness of a home than any fashionable wallpaper or expensive chandelier. How you behave in your house is the true fabric of your home.

"This is simple religion. There is no need for temples; no need for complicated philosophies. Our own brains and our own heart are our temples; the philosophy is kindness."
Dalai Lama

Niki Schäfer

Case study

Sarah is a single mother who runs her own business from home. She works incredibly long hours and has been using her dining room table as her boardroom table and work surface. She has never liked this part of her home. When she met her partner Terry and they decided to move in together they knew things had to change.

The layout of the house meant the dining room felt more like a 'through room' than a room of its own. It certainly didn't feel like the heart of the home. Structural changes were not possible but a new feel was really required if they were going to create a space where Sarah and Terry, and their children, were going to come together as a new family.

We wanted to knock down a wall to create more of an open-plan environment but this required considerable finance as the wall we wanted to remove was a structural one. We had to focus on decorative improvements only.

Sarah desperately needed to remove her working environment at the end of the day. If the family were to sit and eat together then the dining room table needed to be clear. We designed some built-in shelving units on either side of the fireplace, replacing the pretty but less efficient freestanding shelves. We also removed the sofa from the window and replaced this with an ottoman window seat – somewhere comfy the cat could sleep in the sun but, as importantly, with a lid that could lift up to store and hide away the day's workload.

I recommended a warm colour for the walls as a way of pepping up conversation and keeping dinnertime lively but Sarah was not a fan of oranges. I suggested instead that we use a dark yet warm purple (traditionally associated with colder hues) which could be the deep backdrop of the room (this can be the case with deep and dark colours) and to liven it up with bright pink and red accessories.

Sarah loves a touch of glamour so we also changed the curtains to deep purples, pink and cream swirls and added lots of shiny cushions for the window seat. Sarah also painted her old freestanding display unit and used this for more decorative paintings of her own. The transformation gave her a room that was truly the heart of the house where the family could gather and feel drawn in.

What will you put in the heart of your heart space?

Summary

The heart of the home has always been the kitchen and, more importantly the fire. Historically, a separate dining room was created to make a room for eating in but today this room has merged its way back in the kitchen. A family area with TV and seating has also been added to this space and it is now a hard-working combination of preparing food, eating, relaxing and even working. It is the heart of the home.

The heart space also refers to understanding what goes on in the house. It's a space where we can assess each other's needs and see if we can help. It's a space in which we use our heart.

Homework

Your homework in this chapter has been to:
- Understand a current situation in your family and relate it to the human needs as defined by Tony Robbins.
  - Certainty.
  - Uncertainty.
  - Significance.
  - Love & connection.
  - Growth.
  - Contribution.
- See if you can find new conclusions as a result of your heartfelt understanding.
- Look again at your chosen images and find ones that represent social environments or that embody a warm welcome. Develop a scheme (using the principles you learnt in the last chapter) to create a warm and welcoming space in which you can entertain.

Congratulations

You have achieved so much in the past few chapters. You have built two strong foundations – one of personal style and the other in family thinking and together these will give you the solid infrastructure of your home, a home that is calm, sane and outrageously gorgeous.

You have travelled through the seven spaces of your home and it has been my hope that with each space, you have gained confidence, understanding and the necessary skills to create a calm, sane home. Heart space is the last chapter because it requires the most thought. It is a place where we feed our bodies and we nourish our souls and it's been a journey to get to this central part of your home. Now you are here you can celebrate the skills you have acquired and the development you have made in yourself. You should feel proud of what you have understood and everything you have given thought to.

I hope you can see how far you have come. I hope you can appreciate the work you have put in and the impact that it is already having and is certainly going to have in your future. I hope you are proud of yourself and are confident to move forward. In the conclusion, I have pulled the entire design process together so you can truly appreciate what you have accomplished.

Niki Schäfer

FOUNDATION 3: HOUSE RULES & HOUSEKEEPING

Conclusion

"It's not about creating a home that's perfect, it's about creating a home that's perfect for you."
Niki Schäfer

DWELL-BEING MODEL

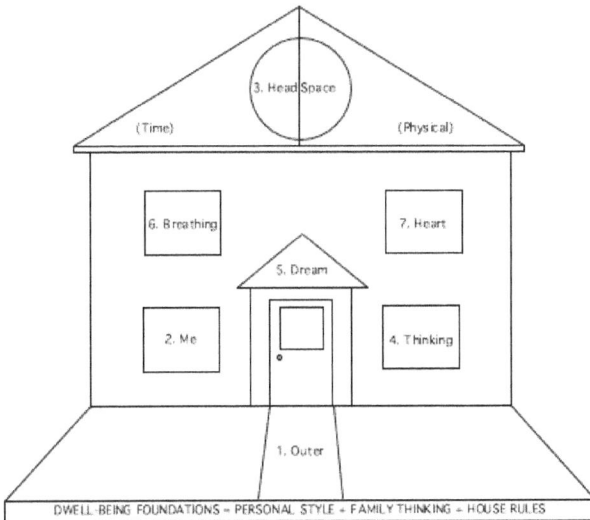

You have been on a long journey through your home. And you have learnt many tricks and tips, some simple, some complex, some practical and some with a hint of the spiritual in them. I'm sure parts of the book were already familiar to you with and other aspects were new to you. I hope that it was all a good reminder to you though. I trust that you now have the confidence to put into practice the techniques you have acquired and the skills you have been taught. This is what you know.

Outer space

There is no point in designing a home if you don't have a firm idea of what home means to you. Working out your values provides you with a solid foundation. This means that when you're faced with decisions later on in the process you have a much clearer idea of why you like something, what you are trying to achieve and the genuine feeling of home you are trying to create. It is so important to do this type of groundwork and much like building a house itself it will provide you with solid foundations and a sturdy structure.

The key to outer space:
Knowing your personal values.

Me space

As a mum, we often find ourselves at the end of a very long list of things to do. Whether we stay at home full-time or try and juggle work into the mix as well our personal needs are frequently forgotten under a pile of dirty plates and school forms to fill out. Me Space is about understanding that you are a priority. In fact you are priority number one. Let's be honest, without you everything would fall apart so it is without doubt imperative that you look after your own needs (*before* looking after everyone else).

Me Space is a journey of exploring your own taste and style and is a fabulously indulgent experience of working out what appeals to you and why. It's a journey into your past, your present circumstances and what your aspirations are for the future. Collecting images that represent these aspects of yourself and then creating a concept board for these to be the basis of your home means that these ideas, the emotions and passion in them, will permeate the house. Your love, your humour, your determination, your adventurousness, your grace, your playfulness, your courage, your joy, your spirit, your sexiness, your innocence and your charm will be the fabric of your home.

The key to me space:
You are priority number one.

Head space

We all have so much on our plates already that the idea of taking on more is almost painful. In Head Space you worked out that you need a little space for yourself. Some physical space which you can call your own and also some head space. Finding the time to think is a skill you can now apply to any project and being able to manage your time is another life skill that will always stay with you (especially if you practise it and work on improving it week in, week out).

You also worked out how to motivate yourself. You discovered that understanding *why* you do anything is as important as *how* you do it. It will give you the impetus to get off your behind and start and it will give you the momentum to keep on going until the very end. Knowing that you can do this for yourself is extremely powerful but you also have the ability to share this with your children. Can you imagine how useful it is to help motivate others? (Even if it's just to get them out of bed in the morning).

The key to head space:
Finding personal space + time.

Thinking space

Having indulged in working out your own unique styles and preferences in Me Space, Thinking Space was about understanding the dynamics of the house. It's a chapter about thinking style by which I mean the style in which we think. We all think differently and, while at its most basic level you already knew that, Thinking Space gave you some tools so you can really break down *how* we all think differently and, more importantly, *how* to relate with those who think differently to ourselves.

Having the ability to recognise different personality types and thinking types is a skill that will serve you as well outside the home as it will do inside the home. If you practise the science of understanding how people think your life will change radically for the better. Take the time to understand conversations you are having on another level and comprehend how people think and you will make progress in your relationships in leaps and bounds. These skills will work as well in salesmanship and politics as they will in your home trying to 'influence' your children into doing their homework or your husband into discussing the floor tiles.

Key to thinking space:
Respecting the thinking styles of others.

Dream space

In Dream Space we started to get into the nitty-gritty of the design process and learnt about measuring up a room. We chose the bedroom as our first room and looked at the various elements required for creating sound sleeping spaces. In part two we looked at our own abilities to dream, to keep our goals and aspirations alive and well and to feel hopeful and positive for our future.

The key to dream space:
Applying the Dwell-Being success formula - COACH A.

Breathing space

Taking the time to sit and relax, to appreciate what we've got and 'smell the roses' for a while, seem skills from a different era but I believe they've been sorely missed. The ability to be grateful and to share that gratitude is incredibly powerful. It is a skill that will transcend through every aspect of your life and Breathing Space showed you the basics in how to accomplish this.

We also learnt how to create a space in which we can take the time to sit and breathe. We looked at the design layout options for creating a relaxing living room and also considered the colours that would help most in decorating this type of space. The bathroom is another relaxing space and we examined how to make the most of this small room too.

The key to breathing space:
Gratitude.

Heart space

The heart of the home has always been where fire is – it's the source of energy, both food and companionship, and traditionally the kitchen has been this space. Today the dining room has merged its way out of the more formal setting and back into this area and we've also added a very modern family zone so that we can keep an eye on the kids as they do their homework and surf the net.

Heart space is the combination of these three rooms – the kitchen, the dining room and the family room and is a powerhouse of energy. It is where we prepare food, where we eat and where we share what is going on in our lives. As a result, as a space, it has to work incredibly hard because it has to encourage us to do all of these activities well. The kitchen area needs to encourage us to cook food that will fuel us well, the dining room has to motivate us to communicate well with one another and the family area needs to encourage us to relax in the morning sunshine or finish our homework on time. In

Heart Space we learnt how to create this space using the right colours and the right materials.

The key to heart space:
Understanding the needs of others.

Homework

Throughout the book you have been given exercises to complete. Some have been quite rigorous, some have been on a general awareness level and others have been simply fun. I hope that you have done them as you have gone through the book. If you have you will have felt your confidence and your knowledge levels increasing exponentially. If, on the other hand, you were waiting until the end for them to be neatly organised in a group then you will not be disappointed because here they are.

Outer space

1. Go through the human needs and property emotions and see how you feel about your home.
2. Assess the approach to and the entrance area of your home.
3. Take one small action to improve this area of your home.

Me space

4. Investigate what 'authentic' means to you.
5. Practise with the elements of style. (Go to www.dwell-being.co.uk and play on the style

selector if you don't want to cut out bits of cereal boxes).

6. Find some images you love. Choose six which are hugely emotional to you and which best represent your past, your present and your future.

Head space

7. Find a physical space for yourself and note the changes in your health and your well-being that this simple decision and action can bring into your life.

8. Write down all the roles you have in your life. Redefine them in such a way that those roles are motivating to you (they make you feel good about doing them).

9. Go through the time management programme and create a school timetable for your week. Become efficient and find time for yourself.

Thinking space

10. Take the Dwell-Being personality test and also assess your partner. Plot both of your results on the graph and see how different you are.

11. Assess your own, your partner's and your children's style of thinking.

12. Appreciate just how different you all are.

Dream space

13. Measure your bedroom and draw a plan. Create furniture templates and move them around the room into a layout that will work best for you.
14. Look at the success formula and assess your normal way of working alongside it. Assess what has been missing in the past when you have not succeeded and also appreciate where you have excelled in the past.
15. Make sure you accommodate accordingly for future projects.

Breathing space

16. Write a gratitude diary every night for the rest of your life.
17. Design a layout for your living room.
18. Find the relaxing images from your personal selection and create a decorative scheme based on the colours, shapes and proportions of the image.
19. Carefully consider the lighting in your relaxing environment.
20. Learn how to breathe properly and find the time to do so.

Heart space

21. Consider a situation in your family and assess it against the human needs as taught by Tony Robbins. Who is meeting which needs and how?
22. Design a space that makes the most of the morning sun, is warm and welcoming, efficiently

laid out and has plenty to talk about (should the conversation ever stop, which I seriously doubt now you have so many interpersonal skills).

23. Invite people to your home. Welcome them, entertain them and listen to them with your heartfelt understanding and your active listening skills. Be prepared for the hugely positive impact this is going to have on all your relationships.

Conclusion homework

For the hard-core exercise lovers, I encourage you to do one last piece of homework. It will cement in the good work you have already done and make your foundations stronger. It will also build the habits of the third foundation – the discipline of house rules and housekeeping. (After doing all this work, isn't it worth a bit of housekeeping, some daily routines, to make sure your hard work stays intact?)

Housekeeping questions

Based on the principles of each space write down a question that will maintain your interest in your home. You need to find ways of ensuring that your focus stays on this vital part of your life. The questions need to spark your curiosity and make you ponder -- make them pertinent, make an impact on yourself. Use the keys I have just provided as a basis but use your own words to create the questions. Here are some examples but please do tweak them and use your own words. Take responsibility for the healthy questions you are asking yourself every day.

Outer space:
1. How do I feel when I'm 'at home'? What makes 'home' home? How lovely is my front door? (It's so important to fall in love with your front door). How welcoming is my home? What are my home values?

Me space:
2. Who am I? What do I want to say to the world? What does my home say about me? How can I reflect my true personality on my walls and on the sofa?

Head space:
3. Am I working efficiently? How's the school timetable looking this week? Am I using my personal space well? Whose yoghurt pot is that in my personal space? (Ask owner of yoghurt pot to remove it).

Thinking space
4. Does my family hear, see or feel the world? How can I explain this in their way of thinking? Can I show them? Can I tell them? Can I help them get a grasp on it?

Dream space:
5. Is everyone sleeping as well as they could? How can I make my dreams come true? Who will help me with my goals? Who will make me accountable?

Breathing space:
6. What do I have to be grateful for? Who makes me happy? What do I see when I'm happy? What do I hear when I'm happy? What do I touch when I'm happy?

Heart space:
   7. How much time do I spend listening and how much time do I spend talking? What is their body language telling me? What do they need? How much fun can I have providing what they need?

Write a list of seven questions (or more), print them out and stick them on your fridge. Focus on one question (or space) every day.

- Monday – Outer space
- Tuesday – Me space
- Wednesday – Head space
- Thursday – Thinking space
- Friday – Dream space
- Saturday – Breathing space
- Sunday –Heart space

You don't need to work 'hard' on thinking about the question, just be aware of it. Bring your attention to it. If you ask the right questions your brain will come up with some answers for you. Listen for those answers.

House rules - dos and don'ts

Do the exercises. Do them in your own time but make sure it's soon. You know how to make the time for this work and you know how important it is.
Don't let this be another book you've enjoyed but fail to act upon. It's no good up there on the bookshelf collecting dust. Put the principles in here to good use.

Do let me know what you think. Send me your pictures and your stories. I'd love to hear from you and would be delighted to know about the changes you're making in your home.

Join the conversation and post your comments at: https://www.facebook.com/ creatingspacebyNikiSchafer

Congratulations!

I am in no doubt that your confidence will be soaring by the time you get to the end of this process. You will have an abundance of skills in your pocket. Not only practical skills to help you design and decorate your home but also influential skills that will help you manage the tradesmen who will be doing the work. You will have re-wired your brain to expect so much more of yourself, to have an intuitive understanding of other human beings – most importantly the ones with whom you share your home. Imagine the possibilities of being able to truly 'get them', to be there when your children need you, to dance the dance of life with your partner in such a way that celebrates your strengths and protects each other's weaknesses. Be the support for one another and an inspiration for others, namely your children. Teach them how to create fabulous relationships and a calm, sane, outrageously gorgeous home.

Show them how to provide so much more than just a roof over their heads. Create an environment that is loving, supportive, playful, courageous and above all which represents you all, your unique talents, skills and views on life. Show them what home really means. And let them take that understanding and pass it forward to their children and their children's children.

"There's no place like home."
Dorothy

www.ingramcontent.com/pod-product-compliance
Lightning Source LLC
Chambersburg PA
CBHW072338090426
42741CB00012B/2830